Other books by O.S. Hawkins

When Revival Comes

After Revival Comes

Clues to a Successful Life

Where Angels Fear to Tread

Tracing the Rainbow Through the Rain

Unmasked: Recognizing and Dealing with Imposters in the Church

Revive Us Again

Jonah: Meeting the God of the Second Chance

Getting Down to Brass Tacks: Advice from James for Real World Christians

In Sheep's Clothing

Tearing Down Walls and Building Bridges

Moral Earthquakes and Secret Faults

Rebuilding: It's Never too Late for a New Beginning

Money Talks: But What Is It Really Saying?

Shields of Brass or Shields of Gold? Re-establishing a Standard of Excellence in the Church of the Lord Jesus Christ

Good News for Great Days

Drawing the Net

Culture Shock

High Calling, High Anxiety

The Question for Our Time

Dedication

Brian Hermes

Our first son-in-law who loves his Lord, loves his wife (our daughter, Wendy) and loves his daughter (our granddaughter, Halle). In his legal practice, in his church life and in his social life Brian beats out on the anvil of personal experience the God-honoring relationship principles set forth in this book. I am very proud to be his Father-in-law.

Table of contents

Appendices

Introduction

Self-help books are a dime a dozen in our generation. Step into any bookstore anywhere in the western world and you will see them by the hundreds. We have an insatiable thirst to stay ahead of the competition and devour the latest "spin" on self-improvement. However, the more advanced we become in modern technique, the more we discover that the best ideas and methodologies have already been tried and tested for centuries. They simply need to be repackaged and applied to a contemporary culture. Consider, for example, that one of the best selling management books of the last decade was *The Leadership Secrets of Attila The Hun*. Wes Roberts simply reached back into the past and brought someone to life who had been relegated to history as sort of a barbaric little tyrant. But, he was brought back to life and the very principles he used so long ago to motivate and mobilize his motley forces into a nation of Huns with a spirit of conquest are found to be appropriately accurate and applicable in our world today.

Or, consider the marketing success of *The Art of War* by the ancient Chinese warrior, Sun Tzu. The strategies and management principles of this warrior-philosopher of 2,500 years ago have found their way into the briefcases and "war-rooms" of practically every business executive in America over the last decade.

Once again, from out of the past, comes an ancient document, a piece of personal correspondence, written by a "people-strategist" to a wealthy entrepreneur almost two thousand years ago. It contains only twenty-two sentences in less than a dozen brief paragraphs and yet, it is the most articulate case study in *The Art of Connecting*, the building of positive, productive interpersonal relationships, to be found anywhere. Fortunately, this ancient document, simply known as "Philemon", has found its way into the New Testament to be preserved for all posterity.

Philemon was a very successful land owner and business executive in the first-century city of Colosse. This letter which bears his name primarily involves two other players, one named Paul and the other, Onesimus. Paul, the letter's author, was actually writing from a prison cell in Rome where he was incarcerated for his allegiance to a new and growing phenomenon called Christianity. Onesimus was, in essence, a contractual employee of the more influential and wealthy Philemon. The substance of the letter regards the interpersonal relationships between these three individuals. Onesimus had broken his contract, stolen from Philemon and split the scene. By the strangest of circumstances he had made his way to Rome to spend his take in the bright lights of the big city. In the process, he was arrested by the authorities on an unrelated charge and placed in the same cell with Paul. To make matters more "coincidental" Paul happened to be a personal friend of Philemon and had, in fact, won him to faith in Christ on a recent visit to Colosse. In the constant presence of this warm and winsome people person, Onesimus, himself, soon came to see the error of his ways and also came to a transformational experience through faith in Christ. The proof of this emerged in the fact that upon his release from jail, his intent was to return to Colosse, confront Philemon with his remorse and seek to make restitution.

With this bit of informational background we now come to the letter at hand. Paul writes this letter to Philemon to pave the way for Onesimus' return. It is a blueprint for building positive, productive interpersonal relationships. In it, he speaks of the importance of "affirmation of one another". Early on in the letter he affirms Philemon by saying, "Your love has given me great joy and encouragement, because you, brother, have refreshed the hearts of the saints." Positive words of honest affirmation have a disarming effect. He continues with the importance of "accommodation of one another" in our interpersonal relationships by reminding Philemon that, "formerly Onesimus was useless to you, but now he has become useful both to you and to me." In our modern vernacular Paul is approaching him on the basis of a "win-win" relationship. Paul also speaks of the importance of "acceptance of one another" by calling upon his friend to, "receive Onesimus as you would me." No dissertation on interpersonal relationships would be complete without a word about "allegiance to one another" and thus Paul proves his allegiance to them both by stating to Philemon, "If he has done you any wrong or owes you anything, charge it to me!" Finally, the writer addressed the necessity of "accountability to one another" in our relationships. This is the missing element in so many relationships. Paul closes the letter saying, "And one thing more: Prepare a guest room for me, because I hope to be restored to you shortly." In other words, "I am coming by to check up on things and to hold you both accountable in your relationships to one another."

There is much on the market and on the bookstore shelves on building better relationships. Scores of writers each have their own formulas and catchy slogans to motivate and sometimes manipulate people into relationships. Some teach manipulative maneuvers to stimulate others to notice us. There are volumes telling us how to dress and how to win friends to our persuasion. Others even offer suggestions on how to intimidate our way into relationships which can become beneficial to us. Still other books imply we should fake interest in certain hobbies or interests of others in order to gain their influence. When it comes to the bottom line, many of today's modern methods of building productive relationships are superficial and deceptive resulting in short-term gain at best. The intent of this volume and the content of Philemon's letter is not just to win friends but to keep them in long-term, mutually beneficial, positive, productive interpersonal relationships.

Life itself is made up of relationships. Each new day brings the need for constructive interpersonal relationships. Perhaps this day faces you with the need of making a complaint to a landlord or coping with a problem with someone in your social life. All of life is about relationships...husbands and wives seeking to build better understanding, teachers seeking to translate truth to their students, athletes striving to please the coach. Life is about relationships and some of us have had great heartache and others of us have caused great heartache because we have never learned how to relate to one another in a positive and productive sense. It matters not whether it is in the home, the workplace or the social arena, we can all profit from learning how to properly relate to one another. Let's dissect this ancient piece of private, personal correspondence and discover some well-worn and lasting secrets in…*the art of connecting*!

Chapter 1

The art of connecting

(Philemon 1–3)

I have always been an early riser. It doesn't matter whether I go to bed early or late, rested or worn-out, I am automatically awake usually by five o'clock every morning and never past six. You can set your watch by it. A few years ago when I was living in Florida, I flew from my home in Fort Lauderdale to the west coast where I was to speak at a convention in the San Francisco Bay area. And sure enough, I awoke the following morning before six o'clock. The only problem was I was three hours behind east coast time and the little red numerals on the clock radio in my hotel room greeted me with the news…2:55 a.m.! With zero success I tried my best to go back to sleep. Finally, I reached for the television remote control and flicked on the tube. Now, it doesn't matter where you are in America or what time of the day or night it might be, there are always two things you can get on television…world-championship wrestling and religious programming. And there they were in living color at three in the morning in Oakland. And, I might add, the world is asking the same question about them both — "Is it real or fake?" Quite honestly, I could not take either one at that hour so I got up and went to the little desk by the window to work on some things I had in my briefcase. I reached for the switch on the desk lamp, turned it on, and nothing happened. I don't usually give up very easily so I began to do a little detective work. I came to the brilliant conclusion that the lamp had only three possible points of connection. I began my investigation. First, I checked the source. It was plugged in alright and snugly fit. Next, I checked the switch. It was turned on. Now, the process of deduction was coming to fruition. If the lamp was connected at the source and at the switch there was only one other possibility. I then checked the socket. Bingo! The bulb was not screwed down tight into the socket so that it was making connection. I gave it a couple of turns and there was light.

Life is a lot like that lamp when we really think about it. We have all known people in our interpersonal relationships who seem to have little sparkle or shine about them. And we have all been connected with others who, by their very presence, light up our lives and the lives of all those with whom they touch. What is it about these people? Most generally, they have three points of connection. They are connected at the source, the switch, and the socket. There are only three connections or relationships in life. Add up all your relationships but they only boil down to three. We have a relationship with others, whether it be in the home, the office or the social arena. This is the *outward connection*, the socket, if you please. Here we make contact and touch the lives of others. Secondly, we have a relationship with ourselves. This is the *inward connection*, the switch. Here we connect with ourselves in order to have proper and positive self-respect, self-esteem, self-worth and self-love. Finally, we have a relationship with God. This is the *upward connection*, the source. This is what makes us different from all the other created order. We have the innate capacity to connect with our source, to be plugged into the power. And there we have it in a nutshell. There arc only three relationships in life…the outward connection, the inward connection and the upward connection. And the bottom line? We will never be properly related to others until we are properly related to ourselves and we will never be properly related to ourselves until we are properly related to God. In short, in order to shine and light up the lives of others in positive, productive interpersonal relationships we need to be connected at the source, the switch and the socket. I like to call it the art of connecting. There is power in productive relationships.

We are made to communicate positively with each other. We are made for companionship. We are made to be connected to one another relationally. Way back in the beginning of the created order there was a phrase that continued to be repeated over and over. The Creator God paused for a moment at the conclusion of each part of His creation to say, "That's good!". He said it about the sun and the moon and the stars and the land and the sea and the vegetation and the fish and the birds and all His creation. Until, He made a man. And the next words we hear are, "Not good!". "It is not good for man to be alone." So He made him a companion, one with whom he could connect in interpersonal relationships. We are social beings who were created to be connected at the source, at the switch and at the socket. By our very nature we are made to relate with one another and much of our success in life is not determined by how much we know nor how high we may have climbed in material circles but in our ability to build positive, productive interpersonal relationships with others in the home, in the marketplace and in the social arena.

Two thousand years ago Paul of Tarsus laid hold of this threefold principle of relationships and cleverly used it in the initial paragraph of greeting to his friend, Philemon. He viewed himself as connected to the source. He was plugged into an unlimited outside power supply. He also saw himself as connected at the switch. He was turned on and felt positive about himself. He exuded self-worth, self-respect and self-confidence by finding his identity in the person of Jesus Christ. And the result of being plugged in and turned on was that when he touched the lives of others he brought a light which not only brightened their road but had a unique way of lightening their load at the same time.

The problem with so many interpersonal relationships today is a breakdown at one of these points of connection. Some of us have a very difficult time relating to others primarily because of the fact that we do not feel good about ourselves. Some have such low self-image and such fear of rejection that contact is never made with others and the light which could mean so much to so many is never turned on. Others of us continue to self destruct in our relations with others because of how we really feel about ourselves. We often "project" what we really feel about ourselves into the lives of those around us. Still others seem to go from one relationship to another never escaping the short-term. Allow me to rewind the tape a moment and say what I have already said (and what I intend to repeat throughout this volume). We only have three relationships in life…the outward connection, the inward connection and the upward connection. The truth is, we will never be positively and productively related to others until we are properly related to ourselves. And, we will never be properly related to ourselves until we are properly related to our Source and understand how indescribably valuable we are to Him! This is the thrust of Paul's ancient, yet up-to-date, letter to Philemon. Let's begin the journey in the art of connecting. Where do we begin? We begin with:

The eternal connection: Touching our Source

In Paul's own words of salutation, "Grace to you and peace from God our Father" (Philem. 3). The writer reveals much about his own connection with the Source in this initial greeting. As he penned these words he was writing in Greek, the universal written language of his first-century world. To indicate his own connection with the source he used the Greek word, *patros*, which we translate, "Father". He saw himself in a father and son relationship with his source of power. The same word is used to describe the father in the old and oft-repeated story of the prodigal son. It is the heart-warming story of the boy who took his inheritance and left home for the bright lights of the big city. It didn't take him long to lose it all, including his dignity and self-respect. What had promised to be a good time brought nothing but rip-offs, back alleys and eventually, unemployment lines. But the story has a happy ending. He decides to get up and go home. What will his father say? Or worse yet, what will his father do? The same dad who had earlier said, "I release you", now says, "I receive you and what is more, I even reward you." The boy's dad didn't have to release him. He could have blackmailed him with the inheritance money. He could have refused him. But there are times when a father knows what is best and still lets us go. He released him but he never gave up on him. When the boy returned with a repentant heart the father received him with open arms and rewarded him for finally doing what was right. All of that is wrapped up in this word "patros" or "father" which Paul uses to describe his own connection with his source in his letter to Philemon.

Father…that is a tough word for some people. In fact, for many it is the very word that is at the root of so many unresolved problems in interpersonal relationships. It is an all too common fact that many have a very difficult time relating to others due to their own feelings of inadequate self-confidence and self-worth which are a direct result of unpleasant relationships with earthly fathers. But Paul is not talking about an earthly father here. He is visualizing himself in a relationship with his source of power like that of a loving and supportive father and son. This is a good time

to pause a moment to ask a rather personal question —
"How do you view yourself as being connected to an outside source of power?" Positive and productive relationships
begin when we see Him as a father. He releases us to do our
own thing. We are not puppets. We are people. Though this
power source releases us He never gives up on us. The very
moment we are ready to connect with Him, He receives us
with open arms and allows us to start all over again with a
brand new beginning. He will become a father and a source
of strength to all who come to Him, especially those of us
who might not have had a positive experience with a father
in the earthy realm. The eternal connection, touching the
Source, begins when we, like Paul, see Him as the paternal
one and view ourselves as sons and daughters.

Paul continues in his greeting to Philemon saying, "Grace
to you and peace from God our Father and the Lord Jesus
Christ" (Philem. 3). With these words he now brings in an added
dimension in his relationship with his source of power. Again,
writing in Greek, he gives his source the name, "*kurios*", which
is translated into the English word "Lord". He not only sees his
source as the paternal one but now the prominent one. That is,
the Lord. And, he not only views himself as a son but now a
servant. Remember, he is writing this letter on interpersonal relationships to Philemon in regards to his relationship with a
former servant, an employee, by the name of Onesimus. With

these words Paul is subtly showing Philemon that we are all sons and servants in relationship with our Source. This awareness helps to bring our inward relationship with self and our outward relationships with others into proper perspective.

Having alluded to his relationship with his source as that of a paternal one to a son and a prominent one to a servant, Paul now goes a step further by referring to his source of power as a promised one. Indeed, in his language he calls Him "*Christos*" which we translate "Christ". For Paul, a learned and aristocratic Jew, he found his source in the long awaited and anointed one, the promised Messiah, to whom the world had been looking and for whom it had been waiting. Throughout his life he had celebrated that high and holy day of atonement, Yom Kippur. In Hebrew, Yom Kippur means "the day of covering". It was on Yom Kippur that the sins of the previous year were covered by a blood sacrifice. Today our Jewish friends have abandoned their blood sacrifices and seek their "covering" through "mitzvot" (good works). Paul, in referring to his source as "Christos" identifies Him as that promised one who came to become a "covering" for all our faults and failures and to bring us purpose, peace and a proper self-image.

What is Paul saying here about interpersonal relationships by revealing that his source of power is not simply some unknown, unnamed "force" or some positive mental attitude but the person of Jesus Christ, Himself. Perhaps this can best be illustrated with a mental trip back to my hotel in Oakland mentioned earlier. When it came time to check out of the hotel I did not pay cash upon my departure. I used a credit card. Think about that. The credit card in your wallet has no real intrinsic value in and of itself. It is simply a piece of plastic. But the hotel clerk accepted my credit card as if it were cash. Why did she do that? It was a forerunner of the true payment that was sure to follow. The actual payment came a few days later when I received my statement in the mail and paid my bill. Until then the credit card simply "covered" the purchase. As such the old covenant between God and man with its sacrificial system "covered" the faults and failures of those who believed in the Promised One who was coming. And He came! He made the final payment for our "covering" with the sacrifice of His own life and the shedding of His own blood on a Roman cross of execution. Consequently, through Him our relationship with the Father has been purchased and secured. It is no wonder our Jewish friends have abandoned their sacrificial system for the last two thousand years. There is no need for a credit card. The bill has been paid.

Paul could speak with authority to others about interpersonal relationships because he was well connected. He related well with others because he possessed a positive self-image and he had a positive self-image because he related to God. He saw his source as a paternal one and himself as a member of the family. He saw his source as a prominent one and thus he viewed himself as one under a higher authority. Also, he saw his source as the promised one and this set him free to find in Him his true identity. This brought him inde-scribable value as an individual and a high sense of self-worth. Bottom line...if we are not properly plugged in at the source the light will never shine for ourselves or others.

Remember, there are only three relationships in life. There is the upward connection where we touch our source, the inward relationship where we touch our self and the out-ward relationship where we touch our society. It is time to rewind once more. We will never be properly related to others until we have a positive relationship with ourselves. And, we will never have a positive, productive self-image until we are properly related to our Source of power, the Lord Jesus Christ. With this thought in mind Paul continues his initial greeting to Philemon by addressing:

The internal connection: Touching our self

Paul recognized the importance of possessing a posi-tive self-image in his relationships with others. What is self-image? We are not referring to such things as self-centeredness, self-exaltation or selfishness. Self-image has to do with the way we see ourselves. It has to do with such things as self-acceptance, self-worth, self-love, self-appreciation and self-respect. It is the way we image or view ourselves. In my opinion, this is the very core of many of society's ills. Everyday we read in our newspapers about problems brought on by such things as mental illness, drug addiction, violence, prostitution and other types of social disorders. These are most often merely the fruits of a much deeper root of low self-esteem, self-respect and self-worth. A large segment of a generation of young people have now been raised with little self-esteem and it is no surprise when they image themselves in such a low fashion that disastrous results occur. It is impossible to relate positively with others if we do not feel good about ourselves.

In his own words, Paul refers to himself as a "prisoner of Jesus Christ" (Philem. 1) and in so doing reveals much about his own connection with himself. As he penned these words in Greek, he chose an interesting word (*desmios*) to describe himself as a prisoner. Indeed, he was, at the time of his writing, an actual prisoner of Nero and the Roman Empire. But, in actuality, he saw himself first and foremost as a "prisoner of Jesus Christ". It is of note, that in writing to Philemon he does not say he is a "prisoner of Rome". Yes, indeed they are the ones who incarcerated him. They kept the watch over him. They locked him in his cell. But they had only a small part in the drama. Paul saw himself as a prisoner of his Source. He was not there by accident. His life had been placed in God's care and control and while everyone else thought he was a prisoner of Rome, he knew better.

Don't misunderstand what Paul is saying about himself here. This is no self-defacing statement reflecting the writer's low self-image. No! Read the letter carefully. He does not refer to himself as a "prisoner *for* Jesus Christ" but a "prisoner *of* Jesus Christ" indicating he is one whom the Source of all power has brought under His authority.

Proper, positive and productive interpersonal relationships develop from the inside out. They not only have an eternal connection but an internal connection. Like a lamp that gives light, they are not only plugged in at the source, they are turned on at the switch. This process of developing our relationships from the inside out is a process I refer to as "being comes before doing" for what we do and how we act are determined by who and what we are. For example, if you want to *have* a more fulfilling marriage, *be* a more considerate husband or wife. Begin with yourself. If you want to *have* a more cooperative teenager, *be* a more consistent, understanding and loving parent. If you want to *have* a mom or dad you consider to *be* more fair with you, *be* the kind of son or daughter you ought to be. Dust off those old words about honoring and obeying your parents. If you want to *have* greater opportunity for advancement in the workplace, *be* the most efficient, hardest working and the most pleasant and cooperative worker in the office. In short, if you want to *have* a true friend, *be* a true friend. Paul realized that in order to have Philemon as a friend, he must first be a friend to Philemon. It is a two-way street.

When we speak of being in touch with the self or being connected with the self we are not referring to a new-age concept of self-improvement or self-awareness. Quite the contrary and just the opposite! Jesus of Nazareth put it like this, "Whoever finds his life will lose it, and whoever loses his life for my sake, will find it" (Matt. 10:39). A powerful and positive self-image does not come from a pseudo, pumped up mental attitude. It results from being connected with our source in such a way that we realize how valuable we are to Him. Now, what does all of this talk about self-image have to do with Paul's statement about being a "prisoner of Jesus Christ"? There is a sense in which all of the creation should see itself as "prisoners" of the Creator. When we are held captive by His love it has a liberating effect upon our own self-image. By the way, everyone of us is a prisoner of someone or something. Some are prisoners of their own passion. Others are prisoners of their own popularity. Still others are held captive by pride. Some are prisoners of success and others of a particular person. The way to positive feelings of genuine self-worth is to become, in the words of Paul, "a prisoner of Jesus Christ".

This idea of losing ourselves in the Lord Jesus Christ in order to really find ourselves is in diametric opposition to most world views today. This is why so many are living such confused and complicated lives. Many have "bought into" the superficial and deceptive message of new age awareness in their quest to "find themselves". There is only one way to find ourselves and many miss it because it is paradoxical. In the words of the one who changed not only the calendar by His presence but the course of human history itself, "Whoever finds his life will lose it and whoever loses his life for my sake, will find it." All of this is in this Greek word Paul chooses to describe himself "a prisoner of Jesus Christ". Paul was the single most successful people-strategist of his day and it was because he was overflowing with self-confidence. He felt good about himself. He had purpose in life and a spirit of conquest about him. He was positively connected with his inner being. How? He was connected with the source. He was plugged into power and turned on so that this supernatural winsomeness and warmth flowed into him and through him into the lives of those with whom he came in contact.

Everything finds the strength to go on in its source. Paul, like a river, flowed from his source. If we are only connected with our self, if the self is our source, then we have nothing more than a shallow self-awareness and must constantly be meditating monotonously or pumping ourselves up like some old-fashioned surface pump well behind an old farm house. Some people today go from one self-help guru to the next, one tape to the next, one book to the next, one seminar to the next. Pump. Pump. Pump. But when we find our proper self-image at our source it is like an artesian well. You do not have to pump an artesian well. You just turn it on and it flows because it is dug deep into the ground and has tapped into an underground river as its source. This is what Paul is saying to Philemon and to us as he talks about the internal connection, touching the self. The truth is we are all prisoners of something and how much better to be a prisoner of the source of all things Himself. This is where true self-image and self-esteem, self-worth and self-respect are found, not in the emotional or the physical realm but in the spiritual.

In subsequent letters to other individuals Paul said such things as "I can do all things through Christ who gives me strength." He once said, "Nothing is impossible, only believe." In a letter to his friends in Rome, he reminded them that "we are more than conquerors through Him who loved us." How could he make such statements? He was connected at the source and thus he was confident in the self. He lost his life in the love of his source and consequently, he found it. It was a growing experience. In his earlier years he wrote some friends in Galatia in 49 A.D. and referred to himself as "an apostle". I can see him now as he sat in his chair and penned those words. Five or six years later he wrote some friends in Corinth and in the salutation of the letter referred to himself as "the least of the apostles." Five years later in 60 A.D. he wrote some other friends in Ephesus and referred to himself as "less than the least of all God's people". A year or so later he wrote our letter to Philemon referring to himself as "a prisoner of Jesus Christ". And finally, a few years later and near the end of his life, he wrote a moving letter to his young associate and understudy, Timothy, and called himself "the worst of sinners". Most of the world would not recognize this as much of a proper self-image but most of the world does not look beyond the surface. The more this man lost his life in the love of his source of strength the more he found it.

Much of our low self-esteem comes from the influence of those around us. In some cases our parents and in other cases our peers. But what is most important in recovering damaged emotions and low self-esteem is not what others think about us but what God, the ultimate source of all power thinks about us. And He loves us…just like we are! When we, through faith, become His child He says the same thing of us He said of His own son, "This is my son in whom I am well pleased". God's son did not leave His throne to come down to die for someone of no worth or little value. You are indescribably valuable to Him. And, when you awaken to this realization you will be well on the road to a productive and positive self-image which, incidentally, is only found in and through the Lord Jesus Christ.

When Moses, the ancient Jewish leader, was singled out to become the emancipator of his people he responded with a question, "Who am I?" No question could be any more pointed in coming to the heart of the matter. I am a spirit made in the image of God Himself and the only way to really touch myself is to know God through His son, Jesus Christ, who is Himself the "express image" of the Father. What is the bottom line in the art of connecting, this power that comes in positive relationships? We will never have self-worth until we see how valuable we are to the Father and get connected through the "new birth" with our source of life Himself. Having dealt with the importance of being plugged into the source and turned on at the switch, Paul now continues with the necessity of being well connected at the socket so the light can shine.

The external connection: Touching our society

We are social beings who, by our very nature, are made to interact and relate with one another. Like a lamp, we receive expression when we are connected with our source. When we are in touch with ourselves in a positive and productive way, this power begins to flow through us and then out of us touching others and lighting their way. It is not enough to be plugged in and turned on if we are not connecting with others. We need each other. God made us to relate to one another in mutually beneficial ways. Because Paul was properly related to his God and to himself, he related to others in four ways. In the salutation to his letter he begins by saying, "To Philemon our dear friend and fellow worker, to Apphia our sister, to Archippus our fellow soldier and to the church that meets in your home" (Philem. 1–2). He sees himself in these external relationships as family, friends, fellow workers and fellow soldiers.

We need to see each other as family. Paul did. And this was one of the secrets to his success. He built a family consciousness and family cohesiveness with those who were in his inner circle. He speaks of his associate, Timothy, as a "brother" and refers to Apphia (most probably Philemon's wife) as a "sister". Paul thought of these as not merely friends but members of the family. In fact, a careful reading of the letter reveals the constant repetition of the personal pronoun "our". For example, "our brother...our dear friend...our fellow worker...our sister...our fellow soldier" and so on. This was not by accident. It is vitally important in our relationships to build a spirit of community and camaraderie. True friendships are really family affairs.

Following Paul's example, we need to see each other as friends as well as family. He addresses Philemon at the outset with much affection and calls him a "dear friend". Genuine friendship is like a beautiful flower. Our relationship with others is the fruit. Our relationship with ourselves is the shoot. Our relationship with God, our source, is the root. It is simply another way of saying what we have been saying all along. We will never be positively and productively related with others until we develop a proper self-image and we will never have a confident self-image without being properly related to our Source of power, the Lord Jesus Himself.

Paul referred to Philemon not only as a dear friend but also as a "fellow worker". As he penned his letter in Greek he chose an interesting word, *synergos*, to describe this unique relationship with his friend. It is a compound word that literally means to "work with". We get our English word, synergism or synergy, from this identical Greek word. Synergism is the combined action of different agents producing a greater effect than the sum of the individual actions.

In more common terms, it simply means that the whole is greater than the sum of the parts. Take two pencils for an obvious object lesson to grasp this amazing truth. If you hold them together and try to break them it takes a significantly greater amount of pressure than would be exerted in an effort to break each individually. With synergism one plus one does not necessarily equal two. It equals three or more. In using this word we translate "fellow worker," Paul is showing us how much we really do need each other and how valuable we can become to one another when we are together. This dynamic power in interpersonal relationships is spoken of in the Bible when it says, "One can chase a thousand but two can chase ten thousand." This is synergism in action. Yes, the whole is greater than the sum of the parts. Jesus of Nazareth once said, "If two of you shall agree on touching anything you can have it." The wisest man who ever lived, King Solomon, put it like this, "Two are better than one, because they have a good return for their work: If one falls down, his friend can help him up. But pity the man who falls and has no one to help him up! Also, if two lie down together, they will keep warm. But how can one keep warm alone? Though one may be overpowered, two can defend themselves. A cord of three strands is not quickly broken" (Eccl. 4:9–12).

Paul was a people-person and realized the importance of working together with others toward a common goal. Effective interpersonal relationships are not the result of competition but cooperation. "Fellow-workers" share each other's dreams, work together in unity toward the same goal and share in each other's victories as though they were their own.

There is a dynamic spiritual power released when two people work together synergistically. Synergism is what takes place when a father and a mother connect in parenting. This is a vital principle in our effort to raise positive kids in a negative world. If parents are not together in discipline significant damage can be done to the upbringing of a child. However, when they connect and stand together, when one always speaks and acts in unison with the other, the child soon gets the message and powerful and positive results take place. Synergism is what takes place when a teacher and a student connect on an assignment. They become "fellow workers" and learning takes place. Synergism is what takes place when a quarterback and a wide receiver connect on a pass pattern on the football field. It takes place when fellow workers brain-storm together and new ideas and plans begin to take shape. The epitome of synergism takes place when a bride and a groom leave the wedding altar to become one. Paul's idea of being a fellow worker (synergism in our more modern vernacular) is an indispensable principle in managing and maintaining positive and productive relationships with others whether they be found in the home, office or social arena. When we are truly connected to the source and the self we can be connected to the society in which we live by not only relating to those in our sphere of influence as family or friends, but as fellow workers.

Paul goes yet a step further in his description of interpersonal relationships by referring in his letter to Philemon's son, Archippus, as a "fellow soldier". Again, he uses a very descriptive Greek word (*sustratiootees*) which carries with it the connotation of a fellow combatant, a comrade in arms, one who faced the same dangers and fought in the same fox hole in the same conflict. As believers who are connected to the same source we are all in the same "army". Problems develop in some relationships due to the fact that many do not relate to one another as fellow soldiers involved in the same struggles and looking toward the same victory. There are a lot of one man armies in the marketplace today. Far too often when someone gets wounded in the battle, it is his "friends" who are quick to finish him off with criticism, gossip or judgment. Positive, productive long-term relationships are the result of seeing those with whom we come in contact not only as friends or family or, even fellow workers, but also as fellow soldiers in the fight.

Life, from beginning to end, is about relationships. It is about our relationship with God, our relationship with ourselves, and our relationship with others around us. God, our very source, is the initiator of all our relationships. In order to connect with us, He laid aside His glory, humbled Himself and came to where we are. He clothed himself in a garment of human flesh and walked among us for thirty-three years in the person of Jesus of Nazareth. He walked with us, talked with us, ate with us, slept with us and yet He was not contaminated by our sin. Why did He come? In order that we might be connected through Him to our Source. And the result? A relationship with God Himself, a positive self-image and productive interpersonal relationships with others.

Thus, as is the case so often, the greatest lessons of life are in the small, seemingly insignificant and often inconvenient "interruptions" of life. In retrospect, I'm thankful the desk lamp did not come on in my hotel room in Oakland at three o'clock that particular morning. If it had I would have missed a magnificent lesson that has enabled me to relate better to my wife and children as well as those with whom I work and play. We are made to shine. But until we are plugged into the source we do not really live, we simply exist. Turn on the switch and let God's love and power flow through you in order that you might brighten the road of all with whom you come in contact. The art of connecting begins with a simple carpenter from

Nazareth who went about doing good and positively relating with people from all walks of life. He is our source. He reaches out to the rejects. He defends the dejected. He loves the lonely. He challenges the contented. He possesses a supernatural self-confidence. As He walked among us He knew He was important as a person and had important things to do. And the miracle He called the "new birth" is the fact that He wants to take up residency in our hearts and impart that same supernatural God-confidence to us that we might see how important we really are and realize that we, too, have important things to do. There is no genuine positive self-image nor productive self-worth apart from Him. We can come into a relationship with our Creator through Him today and thus begin the great adventure in…*the art of connecting!*

Practical pointers:

1. Inspection…Make a personal inspection of the points of contact in your life. Are you productively connected with others in the external connection? How many on-going, long-termed relationships have you maintained? Are you positively connected with your own ego in the internal connection? Do you feel good about yourself? Do you possess self-confidence and a sense of character? Are you connected with your Source in the eternal connection?

Are you related to Him in such a way that He imparts a supernatural purpose and peace to your life? If inspections are good for automobiles and physical examinations, they are also beneficial for interpersonal relationships, for we will never be properly related to others without a sense of positive self-worth and this only comes in being properly related to the Source of all power.

2. Rejection…Many of us reject others in our interpersonal relationships because, in reality we are rejecting ourselves. Is it possible that your problem is not at the socket of external relationships after all, but, at the switch of the internal relationship? Self-rejection can spring from the circumstances of our *birth*. Some blame their relational failures on their heritage and heredity. How many times have we heard someone say, "I lose my temper because my dad did. And besides that we both have red hair! It is in my DNA I inherited it." And consequently, some of us resign ourselves to self-rejection because of our birth. Self-rejection can also result from our *beginnings*. That is, the manner in which we were raised as children. Indeed, child abuse, whether physical or emotional, is at the root of much self-rejection and low self-image. Some of us began life with emotionally ill parents who never touched or showed love or who, perhaps, demanded more than we could ever deliver. Self-rejection can also arise out of the premium our society places on *beauty*. Physical attractiveness is at a premium in American culture today. Since so much pseudo value is placed on good looks, many reject themselves because they do not have them. So much of our modern culture tells us in a thousand ways that self-image is built around being beautiful and many of us have bought into this lie. And the result is self-rejection. Anyone who tries to find self-worth in outward appearance is headed for trouble. Think about it. Sags and wrinkles are just around the corner. Bake your body on the beach and jiggle it in the gym all you want, it is not going to matter for very long. Self-esteem is not to be found in the physical. It is only temporary. Self-rejection can also be the result of *brains*, or lack of them. Some of us feel dumb or stupid because our I.Q. is not as high as others and, thus, we develop a low self-esteem because of it. Rejection is a problem in the art of connecting. Could it be when you inspect the matter that self-rejection is more at the heart of the matter than you would like to admit?

3. Projection…As we continue with our inspection we discover that projection logically follows rejection. When we suffer from self-rejection we are prone to "project" our own feelings of low self-worth into others resulting in the destruction of relationships. The fact is, the way we really feel about ourselves will greatly influence the way we relate to others. Psychologists call this "projection". It is the faulty projecting of our own life qualities and short-comings into the lives of others. We are all prone to do this whether we realize it or not. How does it work? If I possess insecurity and a low degree of self-confidence, I can become threatened by others and project this attitude into them. If I live in self-pity I project a martyr's complex always portraying myself as the innocent victim. If I am unethical and thus have little self-respect, I project that into my relationships with others in such a fashion that I am suspicious and feel someone is always out to rip me off. If I possess a feeling of uselessness with little self-worth, I project that into others and begin to think they are of little value. If I am filled with self-anger and have no self-respect or self-love, I project that into others and frequently lash out at them in uncontrolled anger. Many of us give our true selves away through projection. Think about it and face up to it. If you make a pattern out of putting others down, most generally, the root cause is low self-esteem. If you make it a practice to always be critical of others, the root cause is low self-esteem. You show me a man or woman who makes it a habit to continually build others up and encourage them and I will show you someone who possesses a positive self-image because they have discovered the art of connecting.

4. Correction...Genuine inspections always lead to corrections. How is it possible to correct a lifetime of faulty interpersonal relationships? Once someone asked Jesus of Nazareth, "Of all the commandments in Torah, hundreds of them, which is the greatest of them all?" And His reply? "Love the Lord your God with all your heart and love your neighbor as yourself!" And with this answer He reveals to us the secret to the art of connecting, building positive and productive, interpersonal relationships. It is impossible to love our "neighbor" in the same way we love ourselves if we have no self-love, self-respect or self-worth. In this greatest of all commandments the Lord Jesus speaks of three points of contact. We are to be connected with our source. In His words, "Love the Lord God with all your heart". Secondly, we are to be connected with our self. In His words, "Love yourself". Finally, we are to be connected with our society. Again, to use His own words, "Love your neighbor as yourself". So, how can we begin to correct an improper self- image? We must become proactive. And what does this modern "buzz word" mean? It is the opposite of being reactive. In other words, we must cease blaming our relational failures on others and begin to take personal responsibility. Someone has said that the word "responsibility" comes from two words: response and ability. It is the ability to choose your response. You have it and correction begins when you begin to use it. You do not have to go on in life without positively relating to others around you. You have the ability to choose your response. People with positive and productive self-image recognize that ability and become proactive by refusing to continue blaming other people and other things for inter-personal relational problems. Some of us spend an entire lifetime simply "reacting" to outward circumstance and sit-uations. Correction does not take place with most of the self-help volumes on bookstore shelves. Many of them simply manipulate the circumstance into short-term solu-tions. Long-term positive and productive interpersonal relationships result from being connected not only to others, but to ourselves and our Source, the Lord Jesus. We will never be properly related to others until we are prop-erly related to ourselves possessing self-worth and self-respect. And this does not take place until we are connected to our Source through Him who loved us and gave Him-self for us. This is...*the art of connecting*!

Chapter 2

A pat on the back

(Philemon 4–7)

It was the 1960's. What a time to be in high school! Those were the days of pep rallies and pom-poms, glass pack mufflers and drag races, bass weejuns and Levis, madras windbreakers and buttoned-down collars, hay rides and sock hops, the Beatles…and…high school English! Well, we couldn't have everything in those days. When it came time to do my English homework I would much rather have been, in the words of Petula Clark, "Downtown, where all the lights are bright". My high school English teacher's name was Miss Ava White. Emphasis on the "Miss", if you please. Not "Mrs." nor "Ms." but "Miss". Miss White had devoted her life to teaching high school English and had developed quite a reputation around my home town for being a strict, no-nonsense disciplinarian. Some might think that automatically goes with the turf of never having married and being consumed with the finer points of "the language". The first half of the year I never applied myself in her class. I seldom studied, had a very active social life, and, in my immaturity, sought simply to just "get by". I remember well the day Miss White told me she wanted me to stay after class. I immediately thought to myself, "I know what this means. She is going to give me a piece of her mind for my poor conduct and grades and probably accompany it with a pink slip and a trip to the vice-principal's office." I knew what would happen there. I had visited before. I had been the recipient of his discipline and those were the days before corporal punishment was banned in our public schools. When everyone had left, Miss White called me to her desk, looked me square in the eyes, and said, "Son, you have character. You are smarter and capable of doing far better work than you are doing. I just wanted you to know that I believe in you and am confident you could be an "A" student if you would go for it." Wow! She believed in me. And that pat on the back after class did more for me than I could ever put in words. Miss White and I started meeting after school, not that I wanted any of my friends to know it, however. I would sneak up the back stairwell at the end of the day to her room on the third floor. She spent an hour with me each day teaching me how to outline and to think analytically. She believed in me and she let me know it. In no time my grades soared from "C's" to "A's". To this very day, every time I outline a book or write a chapter I am indebted to Miss Ava White. She changed my life and the way I thought about myself with a word of affirmation, a simple pat on the back.

A word of affirmation, yes, a pat on the back, is an essential element in the development of positive and productive interpersonal relationships. Paul's private and personal letter to Philemon is a case study in the art of connecting. In the first paragraph of the letter following his salutation he uses this principle of a pat on the back as an entree into what was to come later in the heart of the letter. Paul affirms his friend saying, "Your love has given me great joy and encouragement, because you, brother, have refreshed the hearts of the saints" (Philem. 7). How is that for a pat on the back?

Everything has a beginning and all beginnings are vitally important. A lot of relational failures result from getting started on the "wrong foot". Some relationships that might have been, crumbled at the outset through an awkward date or an ill-planned interview. Affirmation is the beginning of positive connecting. A pat on the back that is genuine and from the heart has a disarming effect. It sets the other person at ease and causes them to feel good about themselves. If we think about it, most of us can attest to times in our lives when some "Ava White" spurred us on to greater heights by giving us a simple pat on the back.

The lack of positive results in many negotiations is at the very point of the lack of mutual affirmation by the parties involved. This is certainly true, for example, in the fifty-plus year struggle for a solution to the Israeli-Palestinian situation which has demanded world headlines for over five decades. Think about it. This is one situation that is virtually void of the element of affirmation on either side and the result has been stagnation and stand-off for years. What do you think would happen if the current Israeli leadership would affirm the Palestinians' plight? If they recognized their right to individual dignity and some type of self-autonomy? If they acknowledged the tragedies of the massacres of villages like Deir Yassin where 254 women, children and old men lost their lives in 1947? If they acknowledged the displacement and confiscation of homes of thousands of innocent victims? In short, if they simply spoke some word of affirmation, some simple pat on the back. And what would happen if the current Palestinian leadership affirmed Israel's right to exist within safe and secure boundaries and genuinely repudiated previous statements about driving them into the sea? If they acknowledged the modern Jewish struggle and the atrocities that took the lives of their grand parents, fathers, mothers, brothers and sisters in such places as Dachau and Treblinka? In short, if they simply spoke some word of affirmation, some simple pat on the back. Perhaps this sounds a bit simplistic. But, my point is, a pat on the back has an incredibly disarming effect and can indeed become the launch pad for the beginning of positive and productive interpersonal relationships. There is little hope for successful negotiation in any relationship that is void of the element of affirmation.

Realizing this valuable principle, Paul begins his letter to Philemon with a pat on the back. Before coming to the heart of the letter with its request to receive Onesimus back, he disarms Philemon by telling him how much he appreciates him and what an encouragement he has been to him personally. The lack of affirmation in modern relationships is epidemic. In fact, it is almost an extinct commodity in our "me" culture. Think about it. When was the last time you gave someone a pat on the back, a word of positive affirmation and appreciation, a word of encouragement? When was the last time you sat down and wrote a thank-you note or made a phone call to lighten the load of a friend with a word of affirmation?

We all need a pat on the back from time to time...and often when we deserve it the least. This is certainly true in the home. Our children need our love the most when they deserve it the least. A pat on the back is the best way to begin productive interpersonal relationships.

Appreciation

There are many revealing aspects about affirmation in Paul's letter to Philemon. He begins by showing that a pat on the back involves *appreciation*. He says, "I always thank my God as I remember you in my prayers" (Philem. 4). He was not hesitant nor ashamed to let his friend know he was appreciated. The tense of the verb in the Greek allows Philemon to know this was not just an arrow of thanks shot at random but it was a sincere word on Paul's behalf. He repeatedly found himself feeling thanks for his friend and he wrote him to let him know it. Thanksgiving has a liberating effect about it. Have you told anyone you are thankful for them lately? How about your son or your secretary? Your husband or your hairdresser? Your employer or your employee? Paul let his friend know he was appreciated. Appreciation is the missing element in many relationships and its absence is at the root of many misunderstandings and strained friendships.

Authentication

In the event that anyone might get the erroneous idea that this important principle of a pat on the back is simply a manipulative maneuver in the attempt to influence another person, Paul makes clear that it must be *authentic* and not artificial to be effective. He goes on to say why he is thankful for Philemon. In his own words, "Because I hear of your faith in the Lord Jesus and your love for all the saints" (Philem. 5).

Honesty is essential in long-term productive relationships. Many secular volumes dealing with relationships within the marketplace are built upon manipulation and are often dishonest in their approach to gain leverage over the other party in relationships. Give people some credit. Most are wise to this approach. Make sure the pat on the back you may give someone is authentic and not artificial. Not all affirmations are necessarily authentic.

Manipulation and false affirmation simply to take advantage has no place in positive interpersonal relationships. Learn from Paul. He finds a character trait in Philemon to which he can legitimately give him a pat on the back. He affirms his loyalty, his personal belief, by saying he is thankful for his "faith in the Lord Jesus". He also affirms his love, his positive behavior, by saying he is thankful for his "love for all the saints".

Paul affirms his friends genuine loyalty. He says, "I hear about your faith in the Lord Jesus." In the art of connecting, order is important. Genuine faith in our Lord comes before true love for our friends. We cannot place behavior before belief because what we believe generally determines how we behave. Paul writes these words in the present tense to indicate his appreciation that faith and love are on-going character traits of Philemon.

Having affirmed his friend's loyalty, Paul now affirms his genuine love saying, "I hear about your love for others" Philem. 5). When faith is authentic it always manifests itself in love which is the glue that holds together all lasting interpersonal relationships. Belief determines behavior. When someone truly loves others it is because they love themselves and they love themselves because they have come to realize how much God loves them. Philemon's love for others was but an authentication of his faith in the Lord.

It is also noteworthy that Paul mentions Philemon's love for "all" the saints. He had productive relationships because he didn't play favorites. He reached out with affirmation not just to those who were popular and prosperous, but to those who were powerless and poor. Do you see what the letter writer is doing here? There is authentication in his affirmation. It is legitimate. Paul is thinking ahead. Later in the letter he will bring up the situation with Onesimus.

Philemon's love for *all* the saints, about which he speaks, will obviously include Onesimus, the runaway former employee who is already on his way home in remorse and restitution. What choice would Philemon have but to receive him and restore the relationship? And what choice do we have when we are in the same place? Near the end of the letter Paul will say, "If you consider me a partner, welcome him (Onesimus) as you would welcome me." And when he does, these words of authentic affirmation about love for *all* the saints will ring in his mind.

Recent national polls indicate that the overwhelming majority of Americans profess to have some type of a relationship with God and believe Him to be the source of all being. But these are the two acid tests — a personal belief followed by a positive behavior. Loyalty and love. They are two wings on the same airplane, two sides of the same coin. They go together like Siamese twins. Through all sorts of subtle ways, many modern philosophers tell us that it doesn't really matter what we believe just so long as we love others and are benevolent. But what we really believe always has its way in determining how we behave. John, one of Paul's contemporaries once put it like this, "We know that we have passed from death to life because we love our brothers…If anyone says, I love God yet hates his brother, he is a liar. for anyone who does not love his brother, whom he has seen, cannot love God, whom he has not seen" (1 John 4:20). Their own leader and teacher, Jesus of Nazareth, in His great commandment, said loving others issued from first loving God, our source, with all our heart.

Put yourself in Philemon's place as he read this initial paragraph in this personal piece of private correspondence filled with words of authentic affirmation. Word had gotten out about him. Paul writes because he says he has "heard" about all these positive character traits on the part of Philemon. Can anyone in your home give you an authentic pat on the back? Can anyone in your office give you an authentic pat on the back? Has anyone in your sphere of influence "heard" about your faith in and love for others? Is the word out on you as it was on Philemon? If not, why not?

A pat on the back must be authentic in order to be effective. In winning friends and positively influencing others it is not enough to let them know they *are* appreciated but *why* they are appreciated. This is not manipulation. It is honesty in affirmation.

Aspiration

A genuine pat on the back involves not only appreciation and authentication but it also has an element of *aspiration* about it. It causes us to aspire to greater goals. Paul continues his epistle, "I pray that you may be active in sharing your faith" (Philem. 6). Now what is this effective people person up to? He is challenging Philemon to "be active". Not reactive! But, active. Having previously acknowledged his faith, Paul now gives a word of encouragement and challenge to his friend. He calls on Philemon to aspire to release that same faith. A pat on the back involves a note of aspiration. It should challenge us to greater heights. Think about it. What happens when someone pats you on the back? It turns you on! You aspire to rise higher than ever before.

Listen to Paul's words. "I pray that you may *be active* in sharing your faith" (Philem. 6). Paul's pat on the back spurred Philemon on. It is easy to douse out the fires of enthusiasm in the lives of those around us. Just throw a little cold water on them. Put in your two-cents worth of discouragement. Our world has no shortage of negative pessimists. But how many times has a pat on the back, a word of affirmation given someone the aspiration and self-confidence to go on? Those among us in the business of building mutually beneficial, positive relationships share those things nearest and dearest with others. And nothing can be of more value than a personal faith which produces an endless hope instead of a life philosophy offering nothing but a hopeless end.

Paul was active in sharing his faith and challenged others to be also. Can you imagine winning a million dollar sweepstakes and not telling any of your friends or family or fellow workers about it? Can you imagine winning the World Series in baseball and never wearing your championship ring, never sharing the good news with anyone? And you tell me, is it possible to be connected with the Creator of the universe through a personal faith in His Son and not be active in sharing that faith with others? Paul's affirmation and encouragement of Philemon brought a positive aspiration into his life that motivated him to become proactive in his relationships with others.

Jesus reminded His followers that a truly wise person was one who not only knew what he should do but was one who became active in putting it into practice. Paul is challenging his friend, Philemon, and us, to become the initiator in our relationships by becoming active. A pat on the back has an element of aspiration about it. It challenges us to aspire to new beginnings. It moves us to make it happen. A pat on the back will work in your business. It will get you off dead center. It will work on your athletic team. It will work in your classroom. It will do wonders in your home. When you affirm someone it motivates them to try harder and do better. This is why the most successful college football coaches over the long haul are leaders like Bobby Bowden of Florida State and Joe Paterno of Penn State, men who lead their young athletes by encouragement and affirmation. Watch them on the sidelines as they move from player to player patting them on the back and causing them to believe in themselves. This is why the most sought after public speakers are men like Zig Ziglar who encourage and affirm their hearers with a pat on the back. This is why the most successful businessmen are men who motivate others to be better than they are through encouragement and affirmation. This is why the best educators are those like Ava White who recognize the importance of giving a young teenager a pat on the back, even when he might not deserve it.

A pat on the back is the first step in the development of positive, productive interpersonal relationships. To be effective, affirmation involves appreciation, authentication and aspiration.

Anticipation

Paul continues to challenge Philemon to be proactive in order to "have a full understanding of every good thing we have in Christ"(Philem. 6). Much is under the surface of this statement in the opening paragraph of affirmation in his letter to Philemon. He is "anticipating" asking Philemon to receive Onesimus a couple of paragraphs later in the epistle. He was keenly aware that if Philemon possessed a "full understanding of every good thing" he would have no recourse but to forgive and accept his run-away former employee. This phrase of the letter is filled with *anticipation* that Philemon will do the right thing. There is a bit of a sense in which he is setting his friend up here, anticipating the fact that if he does, indeed, have a "full understanding of every good thing in Christ" this will also include Christ's familiar command to forgive those who trespass against us.

Paul is anticipating the fact that Philemon's "faith and love for all the saints" previously mentioned will include Onesimus who earlier wronged him. This is a big pill to swallow. In fact, you can not know how big a pill it is unless you have been deeply wronged by someone you held within your confidence and trust. Paul believes in Philemon and is filled with anticipation as he pens his letter. A few paragraphs later he will call upon his friend to "welcome him (Onesimus) as you would welcome me". And then he concludes saying, "Confident of your obedience, I write to you, knowing that you will do even more than I ask" (Philem. 21). Talk about a pat on the back that carries with it a note of anticipation…there it is!

Do you see it? Paul maintains a positive anticipation of the resolution of the broken relationship between his two friends. And when we note carefully what he writes, it is affirmation of both of them that is the key. He genuinely praises Philemon and Onesimus in the same letter. We have all experienced the dynamic power of affirmation that leads to anticipation. Have you ever been with someone who talked positively and favorably about someone else in their absence? What happened? You went away feeling better about them both. A pat on the back has a liberating effect.

The problem with some of us who find ourselves in estranged relationships such as Philemon and Onesimus is that we have resigned ourselves to the belief that we will live out our days without reconciliation. If you are Onesimus in your interpersonal relationships, if you are the offending party who has split the scene, do what he did. First, get in right relationship with yourself by getting rightly related to God and then begin to anticipate mending the broken relationship through reconciliation and, if need be, restitution. If you are Philemon, the offended party who has been deeply wronged, receive your Onesimus and forgive him when, and if, he comes in genuine remorse and repentance.

Perhaps there is an Onesimus in your life who has wronged you. Perhaps there is a Philemon in your life, someone you have wronged. Perhaps you are Paul and could be the key in restoring broken relationships. The situation may seem so complex you are at a loss as to where or how you could ever begin? The place to start is with a pat on the back. How do you think Onesimus must have felt when he heard Paul say to Philemon, "If he (Onesimus) has done you any wrong or owes you anything, charge it to me." That particular pat on the back helped bring him home in remorse. How do you think Philemon felt when he heard Paul say, "I am confident of your obedience and I know you will do even more than I ask." That particular pat on the back was the encouragement he needed to do the right thing. Anticipation… it is the outcome of an expression of authentic appreciation.

Admiration

In his letter, Paul relates a bona fide *admiration* of his friend Philemon. He resumes his letter stating, "Your love has given me great joy and encouragement" (Philem. 7). In reality, it is not simply Philemon's love for Paul personally that has brought him this encouragement, but, his love for "all the saints". What is it about this fellow that is so admirable to the great apostle? It is his love. Where did it originate? In the eternal connection, his "faith in the Lord Jesus". This is what inspired his love for others. His giving of himself which cheered and challenged, motivated and moved others to greater service brightened Paul's day across the miles and into the very Roman prison cell in which he was held. This led him to say in admiration of his friend, "Your love has given me great joy and encouragement because you, brother, have refreshed the hearts of the saints."

Some time ago, my wife, Susie, and I were guests of friends at Skibo Castle in the Scottish highlands. It is the former home of the late, great Scottish-American industrialist, Andrew Carnegie. I was particularly fascinated by his library, still in place and containing much of his personal correspondence. There I came across the name of Charles Schwab. I suppose everyone from Dale Carnegie to Alan McGinnis who has written on positive relationships has told his story. It certainly bears repeating in any chapter dealing with affirmation of one another. Charles Schwab worked for the multi-millionaire industrialist, Carnegie. He became the first man to earn a one million dollar salary in a single calendar year. One might be quick to assume that he knew more about the manufacturing of steel than anyone else in the world. Wrong. In fact, by his own admission there were many others with far greater technical know-how than his. Why then would Andrew Carnegie pay Charles Schwab a million dollars a year? And, keep in mind, this was shortly after the turn of the twentieth century. Schwab was paid such a handsome amount primarily because of his ability to motivate others into positive and productive interpersonal relationships. He was one of the first widely recognized motivators and movers of men.

Charles Schwab put his secret in his own words — "I consider my ability to arouse enthusiasm among men the greatest asset I possess. And the way to develop the best that is in a man is by appreciation and encouragement. There is nothing else that so kills the ambitions of men as criticism from their superiors. I never criticize anyone period. I believe in giving a man incentive to work. So, I am anxious to find praise but loath to find fault." Charles Schwab let others know what he liked about them and then positively motivated them to build the most successful industry in the entire world. Long centuries before Schwab helped Carnegie build his financial dynasty through admiration and encouragement, Paul used the same technique in this ancient piece of personal and private correspondence to his friend, Philemon. And, I might add, it still works today. The best way to increase production is through appreciation, admiration and affirmation. Yes, a simple pat on the back.

The best way to give someone a pat on the back is with a positive word of encouragement. Try it the next time you are in an office elevator, stopped at a turnpike toll booth or conversing with a waitress in your favorite restaurant. We touch the lives of people everyday who have not heard a complimentary word of appreciation and admiration in years. Some in a lifetime. Say it with a smile… "That is a beautiful dress." "You have such a pleasant smile." Some of us go months and even years without a personal word of admiration directed at our wives or husbands and then wonder why the relationship seems to be in a rut. Some parents allow their teenagers to graduate from high school and move away without any remembrance of a word of affirmation or encouragement on the part of a mom or dad. What am I saying? A simple compliment, a pat on the back, can make someone's whole day and change the way they think about themselves. It can make your employees more productive in the office, your family more respectful and loving around the house and it can make your friends enjoy your company and look forward to being in your presence.

Listen once more to Paul's word of admiration to his friend, "Your love has given me great joy and encouragement." We live in a macho world where it is not in vogue for men to express their love for one another. In many ways that is sad and even tragic. When Holly, our daughter, was in high school I drove her to St. Thomas High School in Fort Lauderdale where her team was playing in a basketball tournament. I had never been on that campus before and as I drove into the parking lot I noticed a sign on the football stadium that read, *"Brian Piccolo Field"*. Brian Piccolo was a hometown boy who played football a generation ago at St. Thomas High. He went on to an outstanding college career at Wake Forest University and then to the world-famed Chicago Bears of the National Football League. Alan McGinnis tells his story in his classic volume, *The Friendship Factor*. When on road trips with the Bears, Piccolo's roommate was the great, black, Hall of Fame running back, Gale Sayers. In those early days of integration and racial strife neither of them had ever had a close friend of the opposite race. Their friendship developed into one of the best known in sports and is forever immortalized in the motion picture entitled, "Brian's Song."

During the 1969 football season Brian Piccolo was diagnosed with cancer. It was not unusual for Gale Sayers to fly to his bedside between games. They planned to sit together with their wives at the Professional Football Writer's annual dinner in New York City where Sayers was to receive the prestigious George Halas Award given to the most courageous player in professional football. Brian Piccolo did not make the dinner. He was confined to what would soon become his deathbed. Gale Sayers stood to receive his award and with tears filling his eyes and running down his cheeks said, "You flatter me by giving me this award. But I tell you here and now that I accept it for Brian Piccolo. Brian Piccolo is the man of courage who should receive the George Halas Award. I love Brian Piccolo and I want you to love him. Tonight when you hit your knees please ask God to love him too." Did you read that? "I love Brian Piccolo." Seldom do we macho men express our love and admiration for one another. The greatest motivational book of all time, the Bible, reminds us that "love never fails!" We all need someone to love.

Is there anyone in your circle of friends whose love has given you great joy and encouragement? Why don't you go ahead and tell them? Sit down, like Paul did, and write them a note of admiration. Give them a pat on the back. You might be surprised what it will do for you and not just them. A pat on the back is the key that opens the door to positive, productive, interpersonal relationships.

Affirmation

Paul completes this pat on Philemon's back by affirming the fact that he has "refreshed the hearts of the saints" (Philem. 7). This is just another way of letting his friend know he enjoys his presence and finds it, in his own words, "refreshing". He uses a Greek word here that carries with it the connotation of being relieved from pain. Have you ever had a toothache, gone to your dentist and had the problem solved? Talk about a refreshing feeling. Have you ever climbed a mountain and just before the summit thought you could not make it another step. But you did. Then you pulled out your bottle of water, gulped it down and laid down in the grass with an exhilarating sense of accomplishment. All that is in the word Paul used to describe the effect Philemon had on himself and others. He "refreshed the hearts of his friends." I have known people in my own experience who have been the embodiment of this phrase. Being in their very presence is a refreshing and beautiful experience. My late friend, Gene Whiddon, had this effect on everyone who touched him. And when he died a premature death literally thousands of people filed by his casket to pay their respects. They covered the gamut from United States Senators to common laborers and they each had a story to tell about how this man had "refreshed" their lives through affirmation and encouragement.

How would you feel if someone wrote you today and said, "Your love has given me great joy and encouragement because you, brother, have refreshed the hearts of the saints"? How would that word of affirmation feel if it were directed at you? Conversely, how would you feel if you received a letter that was unjustly caustic and critical? Which one would motivate you to be a better and more productive person? During the writing of this volume there came a day when I received eight or ten letters in the mail. I opened the first one and it blistered me and it did so extremely unjustly. It wounded me greatly. I continued through my daily mail and by the time I concluded

I had read over a half dozen other letters that were filled with affirmation. One letter writer indicated she had gained the encouragement she needed to seek to mend the relationship with her estranged husband from a recent sermon I had given. And she had done so! Others told of "miracles" that had taken place in their relationships when they put the principle of a pat on the back into practice. I can not tell you what those letters did for me. Words of affirmation have a positive and a powerful effect. Mark Twain, who left us volumes of quotes and quips, was never more on target than when he said, "I can live for two months on one good compliment!" A pat on the back will lighten the load and brighten the road. The lack of affirmation is the single reason for the breakdown in many relationships. Give someone a pat on the back before you pillow your head tonight.

As I presently sit at my computer thinking about the power of positive affirmation, my mind is racing back to an experience of my boyhood days in Fort Worth, Texas which I haven't thought about in over forty years! I played Little League baseball as a kid and my first two seasons our manager was a big and husky, rough and tough man, and we were all scared of him. He demanded the kind of perfection that a lot of ten-year olds could not deliver. I was a very average ball player those first two years. But my third and last year a new manager took over our team. I remember well the team meeting Mr. Huffman called on the afternoon after our first game of the season. He called me to his side in front of all the other guys, patted me on the back, and said, "Did you see what Hawkins did last night? Instead of throwing home where we had little chance to get the runner out, he faked the throw and then threw to second, caught the base runner off guard and got us out of the inning. Now, that is what I want us all to do. THINK! Anticipate the play." And then, with another pat on the back, he looked at me and said, "Great job!" He affirmed me. The coach believed in me! I can't tell you what that word of affirmation, that simple pat on the back, did for me. I played above my head that year and won the league batting title. Oh, that is not a big deal to anyone else, but it surely was a big deal for a twelve-year old kid on the east side of Fort Worth. Never underestimate the power of positive affirmation in your relationships.

The greatest affirmer who ever lived was Jesus of Nazareth. That is why so many people flocked to Him. The religious phonies of His day felt uncomfortable around Him. But everyone else was refreshed in His presence. When we think about it, He simply walked around affirming others and giving them a word of encouragement and a pat on the back. One day in the village of Bethany a woman came to Him and anointed His feet with very expensive perfume which cost the equivalent of a year's salary in the first century world. Several people began to rebuke her at what they considered to be a waste. How do you think that woman felt when Jesus looked into her eyes and said, "You have done a beautiful thing to me"? He reached down and gave her a pat on the back. Talk about refreshing someone's heart. This is the reason she was later one of the women who followed Him all the way to His cross even when His own disciples had forsaken Him and fled.

And what about the woman taken in the very act of adultery? The legalists of the day had their fingers pointed at her in accusation and were preparing to execute their judgment upon her. How do you think she felt when Jesus stopped them, drove them away, then looked into her eyes, saw her repentant heart, and said, "I don't condemn you. But go and sin no more." How do you think she felt when, most probably, for the first time in her life someone gave her a word of affirmation and a pat on the back. I will tell you how she felt. It changed her life. She, too, was one of the women faithful to the very end.

And, what about the big fisherman, Simon Peter. He blew it for sure. He had been so self-confident and braggadocios. But when the chips were down he wimped out and failed miserably. How do you think he felt when some days later Jesus met him on the shore with a pat on the back and let him know that one failure doesn't make a flop. Peter was never the same again and went from that encounter to become the undisputed leader of first generational Christianity.

There is incredible power in a pat on the back. It should be of no surprise that Paul begins his letter on interpersonal relationships with this significant note of affirmation. There is something about our very make-up that calls out for affirmation. From time to time we all need a pat on the back. It is the single greatest motivating factor around. Athletes need it. When they know the coach believes in them they perform better. Musicians need affirmation. When they know the maestro believes in them they perform better. Students need affirmation. When they know the teacher believes in them they study more. Employees need it. When they know the boss believes in them they work harder. Children need affirmation. When they know mom and dad believe in them they seek to be more obedient. Husbands and wives need affirmation. When they know their spouse believes in them they love better. It is true in any kind of interpersonal relationship on earth. A pat on the back has a supernatural motivating power about it.

Look around you. There are people in your world who have lived months and perhaps years without anyone, any-where, anytime affirming them. They are looking for it and longing for it. Go ahead…make someone's day! Try it this week. Think about it. You know someone with a broken heart or a broken dream or, even, a broken life. Someone in crisis. Someone who is desperate. Someone who is hanging by a thread with hope almost gone. It may be that if you do not affirm them in some way no one else in the entire world ever will.

I know what some of my readers are thinking right now. "I wish someone would pat me on the back like that." But, you are missing the whole point. Why don't you begin to say, "I am going to find someone to affirm, to pat on the back." You might be surprised how quickly you might be reciprocated and begin to reap what you sow. The problem with many of us in our interpersonal relationships is that we are "reactive" and not "proactive". We sit around waiting for others to take the initiative so that we can react to them. And guess what? They are waiting for us! Be proactive. Do something. Make it happen. Reach out and touch someone with a pat on the back.

The absolute master at this art of affirmation was Jesus of Nazareth. He went about His world lifting people up, affirming them early on in the relationship and He continued by patting them on the back along the way. Once in the middle of a hot day He met a woman at a well who had not heard a word of affirmation in years. Everyone criticized her. But He reached out to her, told her about living water and it changed her life. His simple pat on her back was the catalyst that brought her entire village to faith in Him. One day on a Roman cross of execution outside the city walls of Jerusalem He met a man hanging on a cross next to His. That man had not heard a word of affirmation nor had a pat on his back in years. Jesus reached out in His own darkest hour with a word of affirmation spoken slowly through dry parched lips… "Today, you will be with me in Paradise!" And a few moments later He took that man by his nail-pierced hand and walked him into heaven. And, incidentally, those same hands are ready to affirm you today. He believes in you!

Can you imagine Philemon as he begins to read this letter? The opening paragraph is filled with affirmation. There was appreciation. Paul was not ashamed to let his friend know he was appreciated. There was authentication. This was not a manipulative maneuver. It was from the heart. There was aspiration. Paul was challenging his friend to aspire to become proactive. There was the element of anticipation. It enabled Philemon to get into the proper mind set to anticipate good things ahead. There was admiration. Paul let Philemon know he genuinely admired his love and it was, in fact, his own source of joy and encouragement. Finally, there was affirmation, a positive pat on the back. I think as he read the letter Philemon must have sat up straight in his chair, thrown his head back, stuck his chest out and began to feel a little better about himself with each passing sentence. And, I am confident we would feel the same way if someone said this about us.

Everything has a beginning and beginnings are vitally important. A lot of relationships that "might have been" crashed and burned due to poor beginnings. In the art of connecting, the best place to begin to build positive, productive, interpersonal relationships is with...*a pat on the back!*

Practical pointers:

Now it is time to make a conscious decision to put this chapter into practice. I would rather my readers "do" one chapter than to simply read a hundred. What can you do about it? A good place to begin is to write your wife a letter and tell her the things about her that particularly please you. Give her a pat on the back. Perhaps you need to affirm your husband by writing him an encouraging note to let him know he is loved and appreciated. Out in the traffic patterns of life why not give an extra tip to the kind waitress who serves you breakfast each morning? And, at the office, stop a moment at someone's desk and give them a pat on the back. Remember to be honest. Affirmation must be authentic. To be effective, a pat on the back must comply with the following principles:

1. Make it personal...Paul did. He did not send his word of appreciation to Philemon through a third party. He did so in a personal letter. Affirmations lose their positive effectiveness if we ask someone to tell someone else something we want them to know. In short, do it yourself. A pat on the back must be personal.

2. Make it positive...An affirmation is not an affirmation unless it is given in a positive vein. The best attempt some can make at a pat on the back is to say something to the effect, "Well, you have done your best and I suppose it is better than average." What kind of an affirmation is that? To be effective it must be not only personal, but positive as well.

3. Make it present...Paul wrote his letter in the present tense. He said, "I hear about you." Affirmation must be up to date and in the present. It rings a bit hollow and doesn't mean much to affirm someone now for something they did twenty or thirty years ago. Make it present and up-to-date.

4. Make it pointed...Paul was specific and pointed in his praise to Philemon. General affirmations which say something like, "You are O.K.", do not go very far. We must be pointed. We must let the other party know specifically why it is we are giving them a pat on the back. When you pat someone on the back this week spell it out for him. Make it pointed.

5. Make it plain...Philemon could understand Paul's letter. It was not garbled nor couched in any type of linguistic gymnastics. We often hear others excuse themselves by saying, "Oh, he knows I appreciate him." Does he? Tell him so with a personal, positive, present, pointed and plain word of affirmation.

6. Make it passionate...That is, it must issue out of the heart. Paul patted Philemon on the back for "refreshing the hearts" of others. Phony affirmations are quickly exposed and do not mean much at all. When you pat someone on the back this week, make it passionate and let it come from the heart.

Chapter 3

Win-win…the only way to play

(Philemon 8–11)

Most of us have a private spot somewhere around the house where we keep letters from the past. Perhaps a letter of affirmation or a letter of apology written in days gone by from someone dear to our heart. Or, perhaps, an old love letter that has yellowed and grown tattered by the years and is stuck back in a dresser drawer. Some of us even frame letters from prominent people and display them on our office walls. I am thankful we are in possession of a copy of this two-thousand year old letter to Philemon preserved for all posterity. It is a case study in the art of connecting, managing our interpersonal relationships. After all, this is the secret to success in our home life, our work life, and in the social arena as well.

77

This ancient letter under consideration is extremely practical in the "how-to's" of developing and maintaining productive relationships with others. We have already examined the importance of getting off to a good start through affirmation. A pat on the back has a disarming effect. Now, this master motivator of men builds upon his foundation by showing the importance of what many are calling today the "win-win" philosophy of relationships. His letter to Philemon continues, "I could be bold and order you to do what you ought to do, yet I appeal to you on the basis of love…formerly he (Onesimus) was useless to you, but now he has become *useful both to you and to me*" (Philem. 8–11). Paul appeals to his friend on the basis of an ongoing relationship in which there will be no losers. Everyone can win and prosper. Playing win-win with others in the game of life is the only way to play.

Competition

Relationships take on many different forms and sizes. Some relationships are built upon *competition*. This type relationship has been popularly coined a win-lose relationship. That is, some will only stay in a relationship where they always win and the other person always loses. "Bully Bob" plays the game of life on this particular turf. As long as he is always on top, always the star attraction on center stage and always in control he will continue in a relationship. But let the other party win just once and the relationship is in serious trouble. Bully Bob has to win every argument and always be right. In fact, it is not even enough that he always wins, he is not fully content unless the other side loses. Have you ever tried to relate to someone like Bully Bob who always has to win at someone else's expense? He is always in competition.

Why won't relationships based upon competition work in the long run? It is because everyone involved eventually ends up losing. Take, for example, a husband and a wife in a competitive win-lose relationship. He constantly orders her around the house. He coerces and controls. After a while, resentment begins to take root and inevitably reaches a boiling point. All these years he thinks he has won. But he wakes up one day only to find she has finally had enough and she leaves never to return. And, in the end, they both end up losing!

Need another example? Take Bully Bob's relationship with his son. Since he only knows how to play win-lose he keeps his thumb on the boy. He manipulates, controls, gives orders and even uses blackmail with the use of the car. Resentment builds in the lad with every passing year of adolescence. As soon as the son is old enough to leave home he hits the door, never comes back and seldom calls. Tragically, it is not uncommon for him to spend a lifetime without any relationship with his dad. They both end up in the losers column because Bully Bob never realized that a relationship built on competition will not produce any winners in the long run.

Bully Bob meets the same tragic end in the business world. He is a salesman who never lets his purchaser get a "good deal". He doesn't think he has done his job unless he wins and his customer loses. He jacks up his wholesale prices and after awhile leaves his customer with such a low profit margin that he is forced out of business. Thus, when all is said and done, once again they both end up losing. A lot of men and women try to relate to others through competition. But the win-lose approach is no way to play the game. When the final whistle sounds everyone ends up a loser!

Compromise

Some relationships are built upon *compromise*. This type connection could be referred to as a lose-win relationship. "Loser Larry" tries to relate to others on this playing field. He is the fellow with the martyr's complex. He possesses such damaged self-esteem and low self-worth that he feels the only way he can maintain a relationship with someone is to always put himself down and let the other person win. Have you ever known anyone like

Loser Larry? He is to be pitied. He is always walking around on egg shells artificially patting the other party on the back and constantly lifting him up in the hope that, in turn, he will then be accepted. He is a compromiser.

Why won't relationships built and based upon compromise, the lose-win philosophy, produce long term, lasting results? Again, it is because, in the end, everyone involved ends up losing. Loser Larry gives the store away until there is nothing left. And in the process, his "friends" lose all respect for him and they eventually discover that his acquaintance has only given them a false sense of self-worth. Relationships based on competition or compromise have never produced a real winner in the game of life.

Complacency

Other relationships are built upon *complacency*. These are commonly referred to as lose-lose relationships. "Miserable Marvin" can be found on this court. He is the guy who is more interested in seeing you lose than seeing himself win. Yes, misery loves company. He is complacent. He never puts anything into a relationship and never expects anything out of one. Miserable Marvin in basically a loser like Larry Loser. However, what makes him different is that he will only relate to you as long as you are a loser too. As soon as some good fortune comes your way he will cut you off at the pass. "Miserable" is not his middle name, it is his first name. Sadly, he has lost in life and his low level of self-confidence only enables him to find a comfort level with other losers. Thus, he spends his life playing lose-lose.

Why won't relationships based on complacency work in the long run? You guessed it! Everyone eventually ends up losing. Life loses its spirit of conquest and challenge. Complacency sets in and "iron no longer sharpens iron". Relationships built upon complacency never produce any real winners in the game of life.

Capitulation

There are other relationships which are built upon *capitulation*. "Flake-out Fred" plays on this field. He is a quitter. If things don't go his way he takes his ball and goes home. He quits. He capitulates. He gets started but then he stops. Have you seen him around? He has been involved in a hundred different relationships and every new one is *"the one"* he has been waiting for so long. He plunges into it with uncontrolled enthusiasm…for a few days or weeks…and then he quits and immediately starts looking for the next one. He is a flake. It is easier for him to just walk away and quit than to hang in there and make it work. Flake-out Fred usually preys relationally on the Loser Linda's of life, those who like to play lose-win.

Relationships based upon capitulation never produce lasting results. Once again, the reason is obvious — everyone ends up losing.

Cancellation

A fifth way people seek to play the relationship game is on the field of *cancellation*. Here we find "Absent Alan". He simply forfeits! He never shows up and the relationship never gets off the ground. Actually, there is no relationship because Absent Alan forfeits the game. Do you know him? He is the guy who is totally passive. For whatever reason, he never makes the slightest effort to begin a relationship. Obviously, it is then impossible to sustain one since it has never been started in the first place. Absent Alan never wins because he never puts on the uniform and takes the field. And sadly, he keeps others from winning in the process. Cancellation gets us nowhere in the game of life.

Cooperation

Is there a better way than basing relationships on competition (win-lose), compromise (lose-win), complacency (lose-lose), capitulation (quitting) or cancellation (forfeiting)? Indeed there is! Life's most positive and productive relationships are built upon *cooperation*. This is what we call a win-win relationship. "Wise William" knows how to play this game. Paul was the captain of this team and the game plan is woven throughout the fabric of the letter to Philemon. Win-win relationships are mutually beneficial. Wise William knows that when the other party wins in a relationship he ends up winning too. Paul said it…to Philemon, about Onesimus… "He has become useful both to you and to me."

Have you ever been acquainted with anyone like Wise William? He is the man who wins himself by seeing others win. As a husband, Wise William is not in competition with his wife. He seeks the best for her because he is smart enough to realize when she wins and is happy, he ends up a winner too. As a dad, he always wants the best for his son. He knows that if junior has a positive self-image and wins in the game of life, he will share in that victory as though it were his own and he will be a winner as a dad. Over at the office, Wise William is the businessman who wants his customers to win so he can stay in business himself. The most productive friendships in life are win-win relation-ships based upon cooperation.

Cooperation works! It is the only game plan for the game of life. It is the only type of interpersonal relation-ship that ends up with everyone who plays on the winning team. There are no losers. In every other type relationship everyone ends up an eventual loser. Not so in the game of win-win. Cooperation is the key to victory and success. For, at the end of the game of interpersonal relationships, if we do not both win, we lose. Win-win is the only realistic approach to mutually beneficial friendships. This is true whether you are a housewife at the kitchen table, an executive at the conference table or a diplomat at the peace table. Let Wise William put you on his team and you will be well on your way to the winner's stand.

Now, how do we play the game? Paul reveals four critical steps to playing win-win in his letter to Philemon. Step one: Be sensitive. Step two: Be submissive. Step three: Be supportive. Step four: Be sensible. We will see more about this four step approach in some detail in a moment. But first, a question — How does all of this work?

Relations based upon competition (win-lose) do not get very far before they eventually disintegrate. Zaccheus tried to play this game. Most of us remember his story from childhood. He was a rip-off and played win-lose with everyone in Jericho. But one day he saw the light and began to play win-win. It gave him a new lease on life. He began to develop more productive relationships than anyone in town. He restored what he had cheated from others and ended up being the most popular guy at the party.

Relations based upon compromise (lose-win) do not get very far either. the woman of Sychar played that game.

She possessed such low self-esteem and such a damaged self-image she thought the only way she could get any attention was to continue in the loser's bracket while allowing the men of the town to win by using her. But one day she met Jesus of Nazareth at a well and learned how to play win-win. She went back to the very people with whom she had played her games of compromise and introduced them to this One who had changed her life. He spent a couple of days in their village and when He left everyone of them became a winner because of it.

Relations based upon complacency (lose-lose) are equally doomed. The man known only as the "Dying Thief" spent his life playing on this field. Talk about a loser…he wrote the book on it. He lost at life and waited until it was almost too late to do anything about it. But, on a Roman cross of execution outside the city walls of Jerusalem he connected with his Maker and learned how to play a new game. He won! In fact, they both ended up on the winning team.

Relations based upon capitulation are, likewise, headed for defeat. These are the quitters who start and then stop. Elijah of old played on this team. He got off to a great start. He won the big prize on Mount Carmel. The next day he got into an interpersonal relationship spat with a Queen named Jezebel (doesn't that name bless you?) and he dropped out. He capitulated. He quit. He isolated himself from everyone he knew, sat under a tree alone and started to contemplate suicide. When he got to the end of himself it happened…he met the Lord, learned how to play win-win in life and went from there to the greatest mountain top experiences of his entire career.

Jonah didn't play any of these relationship games. Cancellation was the name of his game. God wanted to use him to build some relationships in the city of Nineveh. But he didn't show up. He forfeited. He took off in the opposite direction. However, one day in the belly of a fish he learned how to play win-win and he went to Nineveh and enjoyed incredible results.

The point I am making is that it doesn't matter how you have played the game thus far, you can get on the winning team today. It is never too late for a new beginning! Jesus of Nazareth is not some musty smelling character from bygone days who is but a figment of the imagination and totally irrelevant to our lives in a twenty-first century world. He is alive and can do for us today what He did for so many back when. Each time He would meet a man or a woman He would place them in a win-win relationship. He walked around lifting people up from their boredom, causing them to feel good about themselves and to begin to positively and productively relate to those around them.

Paul got on the team and in his personal letter to Philemon he passes him the ball. He enlightens us to the four steps to win-win relationships. Let's look at them and learn from them.

Step 1: Be sensitive

(Philemon 8)

Sensitivity is essential to all worthwhile relationships. In his letter Paul reminds his friend, "I could be bold and order you to do what you ought to do" (Philem. 8). But he is sensitive to the fact that people can not be bullied through coercion or compulsion. The best way is to win them through consideration and cooperation. Learn from Paul. Be sensitive. He is saying, "I could play win-lose with you. I could be bold and give you an order. But I refuse to do it. I want everyone in this relationship to emerge a winner."

In place of being sensitive in our interpersonal relationships many of us approach the situation with a "drill sergeant" approach. We like to give our orders and watch others squirm and jump. Some actually take pride in this approach and think they are winning along the way. I think Paul actually wrestled with this. The easy thing to do would have been to go ahead and "order" Philemon to receive Onesimus which was, indeed, the right thing to do. But he resisted this approach. There was no command and no coercion. He "appealed on the basis of love" (Philem. 9) with a high level of sensitivity. Had Philemon been ordered and had no say of his own in the matter, what kind of relationship do you think would have developed? It would have been built upon compulsion and coercion, guilt and grudge and would have ultimately resulted in a damaging effect on all the relationships involved.

When sensitivity becomes a lost word in our relational vocabulary we have eyes for only our side of the issue. We seldom try to walk in anyone else's shoes nor are we sensitive to their needs. Paul is being extremely sensitive to Philemon here. He desires a long-term, continual relationship with his trusted friend. Consequently, he is sensitive enough to realize that although he could get his way with an order, he, like Philemon and Onesimus, would only end up an eventual loser in the end.

Paul does remind Philemon that he could order him to "do what you ought to do" (Philem. 8). This is the end Paul has in mind. That is, for Philemon to simply do what he ought to do about his broken relationship with Onesimus. The question is, "How could this be accomplished?" The answer? Step one: Be sensitive. Paul is not requesting that Onesimus, the runaway rip-off, be exonerated for his past mistakes and previous wrongs without remorse or restitution on his part. He is encouraging Philemon to respond out of a commitment to the win-win principle and simply "do what he ought to do".

How many of our own interpersonal problems would be solved if each of us would simply do what we ought to do? Paul has encouraged Onesimus, the offending party in the broken relationship, to do what he ought to do. That is, to face up to his wrong and go back to Philemon in genuine remorse asking for forgiveness. Now, Paul is encouraging Philemon, the offended party, to do what he ought to do. That is, receive the repentant Onesimus, in Paul's words, "No longer as a slave, but better than a slave, as a dear brother in the Lord" (Philem. 16).

Let's get up close and personal for just a moment. Is this too much to ask? That we "do what we ought to do"? Are you doing what you ought to do to build positive relationships in your home? At the office? In your social circles? The first step in developing win-win relationships is to be sensitive. Walk in the other person's shoes for awhile.

Many of us have lived a lifetime with few long-term and lasting interpersonal relationships because of our desire to command or control others. The lack of sensitivity is rampant in all types of relationships today. Anyone in a relationship with someone who only plays win-lose should wake up. If you are becoming involved with someone who wants to command you and control you, you are headed for trouble no matter how good looking he or she may be nor how much money they may have in their account. Be on the lookout for someone who is sensitive. This is the first step in building mutually productive win-win relationships.

Step 2: Be submissive

(Philemon 8–9)

A submissive attitude is indispensable to all worthwhile relationships. Paul continues this paragraph on the importance of win-win relationships by saying, "I could be bold and order you to do what you ought to do, yet I appeal to you on the basis of love" (Philem. 8–9). We become winners in the game of interpersonal relationships by being submissive. Love always seeks the other person's highest good. Paul could have called in some chips. He could have exerted his apostolic authority or appealed on the basis of his elder statesmanship and directed Philemon to obey him in the receiving of Onesimus. But Paul was wise in that he knew that lasting relationships are never built upon competition, the win-lose approach. Therefore, he was not only sensitive, but submissive in his appeal.

Hear him say to his friend, "I appeal to you on the basis of love." Writing in Greek he uses a rather strong word which we translate into our English word, "appeal". This particular word appears 108 times in the Greek New Testament and is translated in different ways. It is translated "plead" or "strongly urge" or "encourage". Paul is not barking out orders like a drill sergeant at boot camp. He is asking, appealing, pleading, strongly urging, encouraging his friend, Philemon. He is submissive in his approach.

In our own efforts to win friends and influence people the manner in which we make our particular appeal is of utmost importance. How do you go about winning others to your persuasion? Some of us waste valuable time attempting to appeal to others strictly on the basis of reason. Others make their appeals on the basis of merit, who they are or where they are from. Still others do so on the basis of such things as tenure. Paul teaches us to appeal to others on the basis of "love". Our English language is so restrictive. The Greeks have several words that can be translated into our English "love". Paul chose the one that represents the highest level of love. It is best defined as "no matter what someone may do to you by insult or injury, you seek for them only their highest good." This love is submissive and seeks the other's best. It is the win-win type.

This is the type love which epitomized Jesus of Nazareth. He could play win-lose with us. He could order us to obey Him. He could pull our strings like a puppeteer to force us to get in step and love Him. But what does He do? He appeals to us on the basis of love. In fact, when the Bible sets out to define Him it simply says, "God is love." When demonstrated in a win-win fashion, this type of love breaks down barriers and cements relationships. There can be no long-term constructive interpersonal relationships without their being based on an appeal of love.

Think about it. What motivates and appeals to you the most...an order from your superior or an appeal from your superior? For example, take the father who says to his son, "I am telling you right now to get your grades up and that is an order. You have no choice!" What kind of motivating effect do you think that has on the young man? How much better it would be if, in love, the father makes an appeal that results in a win-win situation. And what about husband and wife relationships. The man who orders his wife around loses big-time in the end. Those who appeal to their spouse on the basis of love with a submissive spirit always win at the finish line. And, what about the office? The best of bosses do not order their workers to do this or that. Instead, they appeal with words like, "Let's see what we can do together to solve the situation in a way that everybody is mutually benefited."

Love has its own way of finding out what is right and doing it. In fact, it is not a passive word. It is always equated with action. Love is something we do! When we submit to love we "do what we ought to do" much quicker and more completely than when we are forced against our volition to "do what we ought to do." Cognizant of this, Paul is both sensitive and submissive in appealing to Philemon "on the basis of love". This is a worthy model for us. We can excel ourselves and motivate others in the process by being sensitive and submissive, not by continuing to insist on our way with a win-lose mentality. There would be so much more harmony in the home and order around the office if men and women would stop trying to control each other and begin appealing to one another on the basis of love. The win-win philosophy produces positive relationships when we are sensitive and submissive.

Step 3: Be supportive

(Philemon 10–11)

Mutual support is essential in building lasting friendships. Paul continues playing on the field of win-win relationships by saying, "I appeal to you for my son Onesimus, who became my son while I was in chains" (Philem. 10). Win-win friendships bring a bonding, a sense of mutual support. By defending our friends we bond ourselves with them. Taking up for one another is a part of the cement of relationships. It is the win-win technique in action. In short, we should be supportive of one another.

Paul's very characterization of Onesimus shows his unqualified support for him. He calls him, "My own son." He carefully chooses a Greek word here that is a term of endearment. It means a small child. Thus, Paul is indicating to Philemon that Onesimus, who is on his way home, is still very young in the faith and needs support and love.

Paul is now coming to the point of his letter and he is already nearly half through with it. This is his first mention of Onesimus. Can you picture the wealthy aristocrat, Philemon, as he reads this letter for the first time? He is reading along and liking what he reads. There is a pat on the back in every sentence. He is smiling and feeling pretty good about himself. This is good news. And then a name appears in the middle of the paragraph and leaps off the letter toward him. *Onesimus!* "That scoundrel!" Well, how would you feel if someone in whom you had placed your trust embezzled your money, left town and was never heard from again? *Onesimus!* But wait a minute. Paul says, "My son, Onesimus." What is this? He reads on, "He became my son while I was in chains." Philemon must have said to himself, "I can not believe it. It cannot be!"

Do you see what is happening? A broken relationship is about to be mended and the catalyst, Paul, is not only being sensitive and submissive, but supportive as well.

And, of both parties involved. He has shown his support for Philemon in his preceding paragraph by saying, "Your love has given me great joy and encouragement, because you, brother, have refreshed the hearts of the saints." Now, he shows his support for Onesimus by adding, "I appeal to you for my son, Onesimus, who became my son while I was in chains Formerly he was useless to you, but now he has become useful both to you and to me" (Philem. 10–11). Paul had shared with Onesimus in prison and was with him when he found a new life and new beginning, when he was "born again." He was like a spiritual father to Onesimus and therefore, he would stand for him like he would his own son.

Cooperation, win-win, is the only way to play the game of friendship. True friends are not only sensitive and submissive to one another, they are, without question, mutually supportive. Think about your own relationships for a moment. Are you sensitive? Or, do you most generally think only of yourself and what is in the relationship for you? Be honest. Are you submissive? Or, do you generally have to have your own way to be happy? Do you give as much or more than you take in the relationship? Are you supportive? Do your friends and family know, without a shadow of a doubt, that you are quick to rise to their defense. Or, do you sometimes let them down? Start playing win-win with others. It is not to late to get in the game. Step one-start being sensitive of other people's needs and feelings. Step two-start being submissive and stop insisting on your own way all the time. Step three-start being supportive by letting others know you are a faithful friend who can be trusted. There is one final step.

Step 4: Be sensible

(Philemon 11–16)

Being sensible, using plain old common sense is vital to positive, productive, interpersonal relationships. Paul concludes his paragraph on the win-win principle by reminding Philemon that, "Formerly he was useless to you, but now he has become useful both to you and to me" (Philem. 11). What is the best way to play win-win? Just be sensible. If the other party wins in your relationship you win also. One of the reasons so many fail in so many friendships is simply because they are not sensible about them. Some think the only profitable way to play in the game of life is with win-lose relationships. No, Paul is showing us a much better way. He appeals to Philemon to be sensible and realize that although in the past Onesimus didn't contribute much to the relationship his friendship is now mutually beneficial to them both.

Paul refers to Onesimus' previous experience as "useless." Now, there is an understatement. Remember, this was the guy who had ripped him off and then ran off. The Greek word Paul used to describe him as useless is the same word from which we derive our English word, "archaic". It portrays something or someone who has lost his usefulness and is therefore, unserviceable. Then, on the heels of this honest confession, Paul wrote down two words — *but now*! Oh, I love those two words... "But now". He does not try to justify Onesimus' previous actions. Quite the contrary, he readily admits the guy was useless. But he doesn't leave it there. He goes on. "But now, he is useful to both of us. It is a win-win situation for all involved!" Now he is useful. When anyone gets connected with his source and comes into a vital personal relationship with Jesus Christ as Onesimus did it does not produce a nebulous, inefficient, ineffective, useless person. It produces people who are "useful" to those around them.

Be sensible. It is time for a word of warning. Some mistake a win-win relationship for what is, in actuality, a win-lose relationship. Take the parent-child relationship, for example. Often when a loving parent executes discipline upon a child the child thinks in the short term and on the basis of a win-lose relationship. But the parent is not attempting to pull rank in a win-lose fashion. He is building a win-win relationship with the child and is looking long term. Loving parents have their child's end in mind (no pun intended!) and desire them to come out winners. In the end, they want to see their child go through life with respect for authority and become a better and more productive person because of it. What the child may see as a win-lose proposition is in actuality, a win-win. But we must be sensible to see it.

The same sense applies on the football field. When on the practice field the coach is hard-driving and demanding, some of his players might think he is only interested in a win-lose proposition. And they are the losers in the deal. But, all the while, the coach is looking long-term to the championship game several months away and he is a win-win man. He is not pulling rank on his players. He is hard-driving and demanding because he has a dream of winning the championship and seeing his players turn out to be winners themselves. And, if they will be sensible they will see it.

And, what about around the office. Often workers confuse the office manager's intensity as a win-lose affair when all the while he or she may be reaching out in a win-win way. Good managers are sometimes perceived to be hard-driving when their underlying motive is to motivate the worker to produce more. In so doing the company stays in business and the worker keeps his job. It turns out to be win-win if people have eyes to see it and are sensible about the situation. Being sensible, using good old common sense, is a must in developing positive, productive, interpersonal relationships.

Now, how does this all work? We must be sensible. The art of connecting is very practical. We must have the common sense to see that in win-lose relationships both parties end up losing. There are no winners in the end. However, when we begin to put the win-win principle into play there are no losers in the end. Everyone ends up on the winning team.

How does it work? Look in the home. Here is a husband and a wife in a win-lose relationship. He orders her around. He controls her. He barks out his commands. There eventually comes a day when her resentment reaches a boiling point. He thinks he has been winning all these years by being the "king of his castle". But she finally finds the courage to walk out the door and she leaves, never to return. And, the end result? They both lose. There are no winners in the game of win-lose.

How different it is for those husbands and wives who play win-win together. Here is a husband who is sensitive to his wife's needs. He realizes the need of being mutually submissive to one another. He appeals to her on the basis of love. The Bible is on target when it says that love "covers a multitude of sins". He is also supportive of her and she never has to wonder if he will come to her defense at any issue which might arise. And, he is sensible. Now, how do you think that wife is going to respond to her husband? She has no problem submitting to love because it has her best interest at heart. He wins. She wins. They live happily ever after.

The same approach will work wonders in parent-child relationships. For example, take the father who knows nothing more than playing in a win-lose relationship with his son. He has to win every argument. He has to be right all the time. Thus, he barks out orders to his son, often in the presence of his peers. He controls his life. He makes all his decisions. He keeps his thumb on him and uses a form of parental blackmail to get his way with the lad. Over the years the resentment continues to build and there comes the day when the son leaves home for college. And he leaves home alright…never to come back and seldom to even call during the ensuing years. Both the dad and the boy lose in the relationship when all the while the father was sure he was winning. How much better and more beautiful when a father and his son are in a win-win rela-tionship. It takes place when the father is smart enough to be sensitive, submissive, supportive and sensible enough to discipline his son in love and keep the lines of commu-nication open and clear along the way. They both can end up on the winning team and enjoy a lifetime of positive and productive fellowship.

If these principles are good for marriage, they are also good for management. Think about it. Here is a salesman and a purchaser in a win-lose relationship. The seller tries to always get an unfair edge and he controls the buyer. He jacks up his price. After awhile, the profit margin shrinks, the company goes out of business and the salesman loses the account in the process. What he thought was a win-lose relationship turned out like they always do — a no-win for anyone situation. On the other hand, here is another salesman who plays the win-win game with his account. He is smart enough to look long-term and understand that if the other party stays in business they have to make a profit. Consequently, the wise salesman is sensitive to what is happening with his accounts. He has a genuine interest in how they are doing and not just in how he is doing personally. He is submissive and still believes that "the customer is always right." He is supportive. And, he is sensible enough to see that he will prosper in direct relationship to his account. He wins when they stay in business, make a profit and win themselves. It is a win-win deal.

In his letter to Philemon, and to us, Paul is calling upon us to be sensible. He is challenging us to have enough sense in our relationships to see that playing win-lose and thinking we are always winning in the process will, in the end, find us on the loser's heap.

Paul reminds Philemon that Onesimus is now useful "both to you and to me." There you have it! A win-win relationship that is mutually beneficial. Think about who the winners are in this game. Does Paul win? Yes! He has the joy of being a channel of blessing to get two men he has personally led to faith at different times and in different places back together in a mended relationship. Had he resorted to giving orders instead of appealing in love it would never have happened. Now he savors the love and support of both of them. Yes, he wins!

Does Philemon win? Yes! He gets Onesimus back and this time he is profitable and useful to him. And, he gets him back with repentance and restitution to boot.

Does Onesimus win? Yes! He gets to come home. And what is more he returns, in Paul's words, "No longer as a slave, but better than a slave, as a dear brother" (Philem. 16). There are no losers when the game of win-win is played. Do you see it? Win-win relationships are the secret to life. They are obtained and maintained when we are sensitive, submissive, supportive and sensible in our dealings with each other.

Let's rewind again for a moment and go back to the basic premise of our book. We will never be properly related to others until we are properly related to ourselves and we will never be properly related to ourselves until we are properly related to God. Some have the idea that to put on the uniform of the Christian life is to play on the field of a lose-lose proposition. Ted Turner, television magnate and baseball owner, made headlines with his comment that "Christianity is for losers." He is not the only one who shares this belief. People who go through life playing win-lose with others think Christianity is about religion. A dead, lifeless and archaic religion at that. And in many places and in many ways it is sadly true. "Religion" has basically been a win-lose game. It has coerced, controlled, oppressed, obsessed and virtually enslaved people through the centuries. It has been at the root of many world conflicts and continues today to be the cause of much confusion in places such as the Middle East.

Paul is not about "religion" in his letter to Philemon. He is about "relationships" and there is a world of difference. Many people misunderstand Jesus of Nazareth for the same reason. He was not about religion. In fact, He openly rebuked its excesses and perversions. He was, and still is today, about relationships. There are only three relationships in life. There is the outward expression, the relationship with others. There is the inward expression, the relationship with self which produces self-esteem and self-worth. And, there is the upward expression, the relationship with God through Jesus Christ. And the only way to play the game is win-win.

How does this eternal connection with Jesus Christ work experientially? He plays win-win in His personal

relationships with us. Like Paul, He is, first of all, sensitive. He doesn't order us nor compel us nor coerce us nor
command us to relate positively to Him. He appeals on the
basis of love. Secondly, He is submissive. His love for us
submitted Himself to a vicarious execution in order to
demonstrate His love and make a way out of no way for
us. He is also supportive. Like Paul, He will stand by our
side and call us His own son. He will never leave us nor
forsake us and if we will come into relationship with Him
He will one day stand in support of us before His Father's
throne of judgment. Finally, He is sensible. We should be
too. It just makes sense to put our faith and trust in Him.
For, until we do we will never know how valuable we are
and we will never develop the highest level of self-worth
and self-love. And, it is only when we are properly connected with ourselves through finding our identity and
self-worth through Christ above that we can live with
others in positive and productive interpersonal relationships. Win-win. It is...*the only way to play!*

Practical pointers:

Remember, it is better to do one chapter of a book than
to read a hundred of them. We did not learn to ride a bicycle
by reading the manual only. We learned by trial and error.
We climbed on and fell off a few times before we learned

to ride. We did not learn to play the piano by listening to the teacher play for a half hour each week. We only began to learn when we started pounding out the notes ourselves and missing several along the way. The same holds true in our interpersonal relationships. We have to be vulnerable and take a risk to make them happen. The following are some practical pointers to put into practice with someone this week on the field of the win-win principle.

1. Be sensitive…Try and put yourself in the other person's place today. Seek to deal with their struggles, to think like they are thinking. Be sensitive to their particular needs. Do not bully them to your side by coercion, compulsion or command. Win them through consideration and cooperation.

2. Be submissive…We are not suggesting becoming a doormat here. But it never hurts to lose a few little skirmishes here and there in order to win the war down the road. Resign yourself to the fact that you do not have to win every little argument and point of contention. You might be surprised how this truth could set you free. Be submissive. Begin appealing to others on the basis of love which seeks their highest good. If they win, you win too. And, big time!

3. Be supportive…Let others know where you stand and leave no doubt in their minds that when the chips are down they can count on you and your support. When the win-win philosophy is applied in our relationships it brings a bonding and a sense of mutual support we never knew existed. Find someone who is down this week and come to their aid with a word of support and encouragement. They will never forget it.

4. Be sensible...Use some good old common sense in your relationship. Get smart. If the other person is a winner in your relationship, then you win too. Forget forever the erroneous idea that you always have to win and the other party always has to lose for you to be on top of the relationship. Wake up! Be sensible. Win-win is the only way to play the game.

Chapter 4

Burying the hatchet

(Philemon 12–16)

"Let's just bury the hatchet!" How many times have we heard that well-worn phrase and how few times have we put it into practice? It carries with it the connotation of mending broken relationships, forgetting old scores and letting by-gones be by-gones. The phrase finds its origin with the American Indians in the nineteenth century. When making peace they would ceremoniously bury a hatchet in the earth to show that hostilities were over. From this act of "burying the hatchet" comes our custom of shaking right hands when making peace, striking a deal, or settling a dispute. The right hand, the hatchet hand, is used to symbolically prove no weapon is being carried. Thus, the phrase, "bury the hatchet", has made its way into our western col-

loquialism as a symbol of the mending of broken relationships. This is one of the most vital, yet most over-
looked, concepts in the art of connecting. The capacity to
forgive, not only others, but, sometimes ourselves, is one
of the key elements in maintaining positive, productive
interpersonal relationships.

Paul continues his treatise to Philemon in his next
paragraph with a strong word about burying the hatchet.
He writes, "I am sending him (Onesimus) — who is my
very heart — back to you…Perhaps the reason he was separated from you for a little while was that you might have
him back for good — no longer as a slave, but better than
a slave, as a dear brother" (Philem. 12–16). Paul is teaching
Philemon, and us, that positive relationships are not only
built upon appreciation and affirmation, consideration and
cooperation, but their fabric must be woven with threads
of forgiveness if they are to endure in the long term.

The single most important factor in on-going relationships is the ability to forgive, to bury the hatchet, when we
have been wronged. Any relationship that is lasting and
worthwhile over the years is prone to have its moments of
stress and brokenness. This is true whether it be the relationship between a husband and a wife, a parent and a
child, an employer and an employee or a friend and a
friend. The ability to forgive and forget is always found in

the most worthwhile relationships. In fact, the most solid relationships are those which have weathered the storms and buried their hatchets in the past. My wife, Susie, and I have been married over thirty years and there have been times when I have been insensitive and times (only a few, I hope) when I have spoken harshly. But she has always forgiven me and forgotten it. We have raised our daughters to young adulthood and there have been times when we have made mistakes as parents. But the girls have always forgiven us and forgotten it. There have been those times when they did not always obey and later came to ask forgiveness and together we would always bury the hatchet. My long-time associate, David Hamilton, and I worked together for over a quarter of a century. There were times when we sharply disagreed and even hurt the other's feelings. But we have always forgiven each other and, in so doing, continued to move on to a higher level of relationship.

Unfortunately, many interpersonal relationships with so much potential are destroyed by a lack of forgiveness. When someone cannot bring it upon themselves to swallow their pride and bury the hatchet, they are building barriers in place of bridges to better relationships. Forgiveness and a wise forgetfulness are keys to every successful marriage, productive business career, continued church health and growth, and lasting friendship.

In order to bury the hatchet we must remember there are two sides to the cutting edge, two sides of a coin. There are two parties who must play a part in the mending of broken relationships. There is always an offending party and an offended party. The offending party is the one whose actions primarily bring about the rift in the relationship. In Paul's letter the offending party is Onesimus. Remember, he was under an employment contract with Philemon. He robbed him and ran away under the cover of night. No doubt about it. He is the offending party, and blatantly so. There is also an offended party, one who has been wounded and wronged. Obviously, he is Philemon. And the truth is, most broken relationships need a "Paul", someone to help the others see the part they need to individually play in order to bury the hatchet.

Now, what did it take to bring the two parties together and to mend the broken relationship? The same thing it takes today to bury the hatchet! The offending party must come to the table with a repentant heart. If not, there will be no genuine mending of the friendship. If Onesimus says that he is sorry, yet returns with no remorse nor change of heart or attitude, he will do the same thing next week or next month and the wound will never heal and the relationship will never mend. How many times is this scenario repeated in the lives of those around us today? There must be a repentant heart on the part of the offending party.

However, it not only takes two to tango, it takes two to bury the hatchet. The offended party must have a receptive heart. If Philemon says that it is alright for Onesimus to return, yet remains resentful and retaliatory, there will be zero authentic restoration of the relationship. Most often, the burden is on the part of those who have been deeply wronged. The offended party must be receptive to the offender who seeks forgiveness with genuine remorse and regret. Both parties must play their own part in burying the hatchet.

Most broken relationships can be salvaged. I think I should repeat that and this time a little louder in all caps...MOST BROKEN RELATIONSHIPS CAN BE SALVAGED! I am a firm believer in reconciliation. But everyone must do their part. We live in a day when more and more people are going from one relationship to another to another leaving strings of broken hearts and battered hopes in their wake. Too few seem to want to really pay the price of making a relationship work. There are those who, when faced with a breakdown in a relationship simply junk it. In place of finding the problem and making some repairs, they junk it. It doesn't matter how much has been invested in it previously ... they junk it. We do not do that with our automobiles. We make an investment in a car and if it doesn't start in the morning what do we do? Junk it?

No! If we can't fix it ourselves, we call for help. We find the problem and get it fixed. We have too big of an investment in it to just junk it. If that is good sense for auto repairs it ought to be good sense for interpersonal relationships. Too many make too many deposits of love and time in relationships to walk off and leave them when we have trouble getting them going on a particular morning. If we can't fix them ourselves, we shouldn't be too proud to get some help!

In broken relationships our general tendency is to identify ourselves at the offended party each time. And, this is exactly why some of us live a lifetime with broken relationships strewn in our paths. Few of us want to admit we are the offending party. Few of us want to take personal responsibility. We have been programmed since childhood to point the finger at someone else. But, could there be a little of Onesimus in all of us? Could it be that we have something to learn from him today regarding burying the hatchet and mending broken relationships?

Burying the hatchet involves a repentant heart on the part of the offending party. Onesimus went back! And, he did so with sincere remorse and regret. It also involves a receptive heart on the part of the offended party. Philemon received him and the party began. Are you an Onesimus? Do you need to go back to admit you were wrong where before you insisted you were right? Are you a Philemon? Do you need to forgive someone and forget it? Is their a hatchet that needs to be buried? Paul makes plain the way in this ancient, yet so up to date, letter.

The offending party

Every broken relationship has an offending party. Burying the hatchet calls for a repentant heart on their part. That is, a change of mind, a turnaround, a going back to a somebody to make a wrong right. Paul puts it like this to Philemon…"I am sending him — who is my very heart — back to you. I would have liked to keep him with me so that he could take your place in helping me while I am in chains for the gospel" (Philem. 12–13).

Onesimus is the offending party. But, now Onesimus and Paul are of one "heart". They are of one mind. They are together. And Onesimus is going back. He had previously wronged Philemon. Now that Christ had transformed his life, he had no option but to go back. The Greek word for repentance literally means, "to change one's mind." Onesimus has changed his mind about his actions of the past and is now on his way back to make his wrongs right. He is not on his way home to argue his case. He is going back to bury the hatchet. Some of us go back to others in hopes of reconciliation only to discover when we get there we are still trying to justify past actions and argue our case. Not Onesimus. He is taking responsibility as the offending party.

Reconciliation does not take place without someone acknowledging their wrong and going back to make it right. The greatest short story ever told was at this very point. It is the old and oft repeated story known as, "the prodigal son." The prodigal was the offending party. He skipped out on his dad. Later he "came to himself" and returned home with a repentant heart. And his dad? He was certainly the offended party but he greeted the boy with a receptive heart. They buried the hatchet and both of them went on with life together. Onesimus, like the prodigal son, is on his way home. He doesn't send a word of apology back to Philemon through someone else. He is going back himself.

Relationships based upon the solid foundation of being properly related to our source, Jesus Christ, are not out to help us escape our past and run from it, but to help us face our past and live above it. Having become profitably connected to his source and himself, Onesimus is now seeking to become connected again to his friend, Philemon. He is returning as the offending party to face the consequences of what he did and seek to make right his previous wrong.

We might have a different ending to our story had Onesimus received counsel from some "professionals" today instead of from Paul. Some today would have listened to his story and offered him counsel which says, "Look, forget about your past. You can find justification in what you did. Go on with your life. Try to learn from your mistakes. Forget Philemon." And, had he taken this counsel, he would have lived out the rest of his days, like some do today, with something left unfinished, like a dark cloud always hanging over his head. That is no way to live a positive, productive and purposeful life.

Often, the way forward is back. Back — to admit I am wrong where before I had insisted I was right. Back — to make a previous wrong right. Yes, the way forward is often back. This is one of the great paradoxes found when we are connected with Jesus Christ. In His economy, the way up is down and the way down is up. Paul describes this present paradox as the way forward is back. He writes to Philemon, "I am sending him — who is my very heart — back to you" (Philem. 12) It was at this very point of illustrating the "way forward is back" principle that Jesus said, "If you are offering your gift at the altar and there remember that your brother has something against you — leave your gift there in front of the altar — first go and be reconciled to your brother, *then* come and offer your gift." Do you see it? It is one of life's great principles…the way forward is back!

Could this be the point of frustration with some of us? That is, we are trying to go on, to go forward, but something is left undone and we have not yet gone back? We have not gone back with genuine remorse to say, "I am sorry. I was wrong." It may be that until we go back we will never make much forward progress and spend our days running into dead-ends, cul-de-sacs or zooming around traffic circles instead of making forward progress on the freeways of life. Only Hollywood movies can be successful with the principle that "love means never having to say you are sorry." In real life no relationships can succeed on that premise. Those who enjoy the most profitable long-term relationships are the ones who know what it is to say, "I am sorry. Please forgive me."

Onesimus gives us hope. Look at him before anyone of us become convinced that our particular case is hopeless. There is hope for any of us who will admit to being the offending party. When we do, we join Onesimus in some pretty good company. Moses, the highly revered emancipator of the Jewish people, was a murderer. He discovered the way forward is back. And, he went back and in so doing led his people to the promised land. What about King David. Now, we are talking about an offending party here! He stole the affection of another man's wife, got her pregnant and even assented to the man's death. But later, plagued with remorse, he discovered the way forward is back. If any of us doubt the sincerity of his repentance we need but read his fifty-first psalm. And, don't forget Jonah. He was the original Onesimus. He shook his fist in the face of God and later in a fish's belly found out that the way forward is back. He received a second chance and God used him in a greater way than ever. We can not leave the subject of the second chance without a mention of Simon Peter, the big fisherman. He was certainly the offending party. He blew it in his own relationships. But like those before him, he discovered the life changing principle that the way forward is back. He went back and then did he ever go forward from there! (Read the book of Acts in the New Testament to find out.) When we go back God forgives. And when God forgives, He forgets and His followers go on to their greatest days after finding forgiveness. The way forward is still back!

Who gets the ball of reconciliation rolling? Both sides must do their part. There must be a repentant heart on the part of the offending party and a receptive heart on the part of the offended party. Relational difficulties often persist when we who are the offending parties become to blind to our own abuses we never admit we did anything wrong. Many broken relationships are never mended because neither side will take any personal responsibility. We spend our days futilely seeking to justify our actions and eventually beginning to believe our lie. Consequently, some of us live out our days with things unfinished. The hatchet of broken interpersonal relationships will never be buried unless there is genuine repentance on the part of the offending party. The way forward is back.

The offended party

Every broken relationship has an offended party. Burying the hatchet calls for a receptive part on their part. That is, a heart that is void of the spirit of retaliation or resentment. In the broken relationship under our consideration, Philemon plays this part. He is the offended party. The rift in the relationship did not necessarily occur because of anything he did. However, the ball of reconciliation is now in his court. Will he receive Onesimus back in a retaliatory way? Or, even worse, with pent-up resentment?

Many reconciliations never take place because the ones who have been wronged can not bring themselves to accept nor receive the offending party even when they return with genuine remorse, regret and repentance. Hatchets are never buried until the offended party receives the one who has wronged him with a truly forgiving heart.

Philemon had a veritable opportunity for revenge and retaliation. In fact, by Roman law, Onesimus' crime was punishable by death. Here was an opportunity for retaliation and revenge. And, at the very least, here was an opportunity for some good old-fashioned self-inflicted resentment. Philemon had been wronged, and, by a trusted confidant. In the end, reconciliation between these two men took place in large part because Philemon had a receptive heart which was void of retaliation or resentment.

In regards to his receiving Onesimus back into good graces, Paul writes to Philemon saying, "But I did not want to do anything without your consent, so that any favor you do will be spontaneous and not forced" (Philem. 14). Paul could have ordered the two to mend the broken relationship. He could have pulled his apostolic authority on them. But, he was wise enough to realize there can be no true reconciliation that is manipulated, coerced or forced. It must be voluntary. It must issue out of a willing heart. It results from common consent not controlled coercion.

Paul was desirous that Philemon's response would be, in his words, "spontaneous". That is, voluntary and of his own free will. Forced and manipulated reconciliations actually drive people farther apart and lead to increased resentment. They never lead to true reconciliations. There are those who through manipulated means seek to orchestrate reconciliations with hidden agendas for their own self profit and pride. But they are inevitably found out. Reconciliations that last are those not forced but "spontaneous", voluntary, issuing out of the heart with pure motives. Hatchets are never completely buried unless they are done so voluntarily.

Paul continues his letter saying, "Perhaps the reason he was separated from you for a little while was that you might have him back for good" (Philem. 15). Wow! Now there is a thought! Something good can result even out of bad experiences. The sentence begins with a thought provoking word…"Perhaps." Paul is saying, "Just think about it a moment." He is asking, "Could it be?" "Perhaps it happened for a reason." This is the truth from our Source, the Creator God, revealed through His prophet Isaiah saying, "For my thoughts are not your thoughts, neither are your ways my ways…As the heavens are higher than the earth, so are my ways higher than your ways and my thoughts than your thoughts" (Is. 55: 8–9). Paul is not being presumptuous with his "perhaps" to Philemon. He is simply allowing room for something good to emerge out of what began as something bad. Is it possible that there is a "perhaps" in your own experience?

The beautiful thing about burying the hatchet and mending broken relationships is that they can become productive learning experiences which ultimately result in our own good and God's glory. Don't misunderstand Paul's purpose here. He is in no way condoning Onesimus' past actions. He is showing that we can triumph, even over our wrongs and past mistakes, when we each play our respective parts in reconciliation.

When we read these words — "Perhaps the reason he was separated from you for a little while was that you might have him back for good" — we are reminded of the story of Joseph and his estrangement from his brothers. Andrew Lloyd Webber, of "Phantom of the Opera" fame, has brought this ancient story to life in his Broadway production, "Joseph and His Amazing Technicolor Dreamcoat." Most of us know the story well. His brothers, filled with jealously and resentment, sold him to some nomads in a caravan in route to Egypt. They lied to his father by telling him they had found Joseph's many colored coat soaked in blood and he had no doubt been consumed by a wild animal. Meanwhile, back in Egypt, through a series of events Joseph went from a prison to the palace to become the prime minister of the most progressive nation in the world by the time he was thirty years of age. Famine came to Israel and eventually brought these brothers to Egypt in hopes of finding food. When confronted with their long-lost brother they became filled with remorse and regret and, in the end, a beautiful reconciliation took place.

The brothers were the offending party. Joseph was the offended party. The rift in the relationship had gone on for years and years. The brothers were full of repentance.

Now the ball was in Joseph's court. How would he respond after all those years of being wronged and living with the consequences? From the human standpoint most of what happened to him was bad. He was the key to reconciliation. When he revealed himself to his brothers, he said, "Do not be distressed and do not be angry with yourselves for selling me here, because God sent me ahead of you to save lives (Gen. 45:5) …You intended to harm me, but God intended it for good to accomplish what is now being done" (Gen. 50:20). God allowed it…and for a reason! Yes, as Paul says, "Perhaps the reason he was separated from you for a little while was that you might have him back for good." Is it possible that there is a "perhaps" written across your own experience?

It is at this very point that we are reminded of what Paul wrote in another one of his ancient letters to his friends in Rome. He reminded them, and us, of an important truth when he said, "And we know that in all things God works for the good of those who love Him, who have been called according to His purpose" (Rom. 8:28). This is *confidential*. He says, "*We* know." This truth is not understood by a world that is not connected at the Source. It is a family secret known to those in the family. This truth is also *constructive*. Yes, "things work together for good." Not every thing that happens is good. Onesimus' actions which resulted in his broken relationship with Philemon were not good. But God can take even bad things and work them together for our good. It is also *comprehensive*. Look again, "*all* things are working for good." I hate the taste of baking soda by itself. I would never think about sitting down to eat a bowl of flour. But when you put them together and make some biscuits…now I can go for that. Unpleasant things can "work together" for good. This truth is also *conditional*. It only works for those "who love God and are called according to His purpose." If we are the offending party our purpose is to repent with remorse and regret. If we are the offended party our purpose is to receive without revenge or resentment. Yes, "Perhaps the reason he was separated from you for a little while was that you might have him back for good" (Philem. 15).

Most often when we are in the midst of great difficulty it is hard to see any good in it at all. It is for this very reason that I love Paul's use of the words — "for a little while." Difficulties are temporary. Broken relationships can be too! The most repeated phrase in the Bible is, "And it came to pass!" Most of our difficulties have a way of passing. We can all think of past experiences which, when we were in the midst of them, were so bad, yet, looking back in retrospect, turned out for our good. Perhaps the reason you, too, were separated from something or someone for a little while was that you might win in the end.

Paul continues his appeal to Philemon, the offended party, saying, "have him back...no longer as a slave, but better than a slave, as a dear brother. He is very dear to me but even dearer to you, both as a man and as a brother in the Lord" (Philem. 15–16).

What is the moral here? There is often a deeper relationship *after* reconciliation than there was before. The offended party does not soon forget the humility and repentance of the offending party. And, the offending party does not soon forget the forgiving and receptive heart of the offended party. Therefore, there can be a deeper and more appreciative love toward one another. Thus Paul writes, "Perhaps the reason he was separated from you for a while was that you might have him back for good — no longer as a slave, but as a dear brother. He is very dear to me *but even dearer to you* both as a man and a brother."

Philemon had a receptive heart toward Onesimus. His reception of him "as a man" points to reinstating him to his previous position. Onesimus will be a better employee in the future because of his second chance. But that is not all. He is also returning as a "brother." But, even more — "as a dear brother." This new position is what lifts us all to a higher and more productive relationship as "brothers" because we are both plugged into the same source.

The new and closer relationship we can enjoy with one

another through Jesus Christ does not free us from previous obligations and responsibilities. Paul is not asking, nor suggesting, that Philemon free Onesimus from his prior commitments or obligations. He is opening Philemon's eyes to a totally new relationship. On the socio-economic level things might well remain the same between the two individuals. But, on the spiritual level they would become equals, "brothers". It is important that Paul is stressing our worth and dignity as individuals as well as followers of Christ. Here is respect and the observation of basic human dignity in our relationships.

Our interpersonal relationships are changed for the better when they are changed from within by the love and power we find in being plugged into our source, Jesus Christ. We will never know mended relationships on the highest level until we each are properly connected to our source. I think it is time to rewind the tape once more. We will never be properly related to one another until we are properly related to ourselves and we will never exhibit a healthy sense of self-worth and self-esteem until we are properly connected to our Source of power and love, the Lord Jesus Christ.

Leonardo da Vinci, the famous artist best known for his depiction of "The Last Supper", epitomizes the value of mended relationships and buried hatchets. While most of us are familiar with his famous painting of our Lord's last meal in the upper room, few have ever heard the real story behind the story. While in the process of painting his masterpiece he had a brutal and bitter altercation with a fellow painter. The master was so enraged that he began to plot an evil scheme. He would paint the face of his own adversary into the face of Judas and thus portray him to all posterity as the traitor himself. As soon as da Vinci finished painting Judas everyone immediately recognized him as Leonardo's former friend. He continued to paint the Lord's Supper scene adding each of the disciples into the portrait. It then came time to paint the face of Christ. However, as much as he tried, one attempt after another, he could not paint the Lord's face. Something was strangely keeping him from it. His own heart revealed to him that his hatred for his fellow painter was the problem. He buried the hatchet with his friend, repainted Judas' face with another, and then, with great liberty, painted the face of Christ and, thus, completed the masterpiece we have admired down through the centuries.

Reconciliation only takes place when both the offending and the offended parties do their respective parts. Quite honestly, the problem with some of us who are offended is not that we retaliate but that we harbor resentment. And, the truth is, this is much more deadly. The most devastating effect of resentment is not what it does to others, but, what it does to us. It will damage us physically. Harboring hatred in the heart can have a damaging effect on such things as blood pressure and normal bodily functions. Many who have been eaten up with resentment have also found they were soon eaten up with ulcers as well. It has a damaging effect upon us physically.

Resentment has a depressing effect upon us mentally. When it consumes us it can warp our capacity to think right. Many people suffer from mental and emotional problems for the simple fact that they harbor deep resentment toward others and have never forgiven past wrongs even though the offending parties have returned in genuine remorse. Resentment has its own diabolic way of damaging us physically and depressing us mentally.

But there is more. It also debilitates us spiritually. None of us can effectively pray or read our Bibles when we harbor hatred or resentment toward someone else. Once Jesus said, "When you stand praying, if you hold anything against anyone, forgive him, so that your Father in heaven may forgive you your sins" (Mark 11:25). One of the most dangerous things about broken relationships is the effect they can have on the offended party who will not bury the hatchet with the offending party. It damages us physically, depresses us mentally and debilitates us spiritually. Relationally speaking, the way forward is always back. It is at this very point that, in another letter, Paul challenges his friends at Ephesus to, " Get rid of all bitterness, rage and anger, brawling and slander, along with every form of malice. Be kind and compassionate to one another, forgiving each other, just as in Christ God forgave you" (Eph. 4:31–32).

In our macho world a lot of people have a warped image of the offended party who forgives and forgets and begins again. His caricature in the minds of many is of one who is weak and wimpy. However, just the opposite is true. Forgiveness is a positive and powerful force and it takes a strong person to forgive. Anyone can harbor resentment with an unforgiving spirit. It doesn't take any strength at all. But, it takes a strong man or woman to be big enough to say, "I forgive you. And, what is more, I will forget it. Let's begin again!"

Think for a moment about the individuals who have had the greatest impact upon your life. As I think about it, four or five people surface in my mind. My dad and mom are two of them. They surrounded me with love. They instilled self-confidence within me causing me to believe my reach could always exceed my grasp. I never remember them missing one of my ball games. They were always "there" for me. I think of my wife, Susie. No one knows quite like

I what an incredible individual she really is. For over thirty years we have been "one" — physically, emotionally, spiritually, parentally — in the most wonderful sense imaginable. My mentor, Fred Swank, comes quickly to mind. He was a people person extraordinaire. He was like a second father to me. He loved me and gave me his most valuable possession, his time. Although he is no longer with us physically, seldom does a day go by that I do not put into practice something he taught me about relationships.

As I think about these particular people, it dawns on me that they all have one thing in common. It isn't just that they believed in me and encouraged me. But, they each in their own unique way, forgave me of my faults. Yes, they forgave me and they forgot it! There were more times than I like to remember when I rebelled against my father. But, he always forgave me and never brought it up again. As many times as I have let Susie down, she has always forgiven me and forgotten it. The same holds true with Dr. Swank. I made a lot of mistakes under his tutorship and supervision but he always forgave me and helped me learn from those very mistakes so they would not be made again. Forgiveness has a dynamic power about it in the lives of others. There is something about it that brings out the best in us, regardless of whether we are on the giving or receiving end.

Reconciliation was set into motion with Philemon and

his estranged friend, Onesimus, because both of them did their part in burying the hatchet. Onesimus returned with a repentant heart and Philemon, in turn, received him with a receptive heart. Often the pieces of broken relationships are never put back together because as much as the offending party would like to see them mended, the offended party is so filled with retaliation, revenge or resentment they can not bring themselves to truly forgive much less forget.

On the surface one might think the key to reconciliation lies with the offending party. Not really. In most cases a genuine burying of the hatchet awaits the offended parties' ability to forgive and forget previous wrongs.

We are talking about relationships here. This is what life is all about. The most important key in on-going positive, productive interpersonal relationships is the ability to forgive. In fact, the strongest lifetime relationships are the ones who know what it is to repent and receive, to forgive and forget.

Philemon and Onesimus have been on center stage in this relationship drama. However, there is one person who plays a major part in their reconciliation. Look at Paul. He is the reconciler. He stands in the middle with Onesimus (the offending party) in one hand and Philemon (the offended party) in the other. And, he brings them together.

And so, one with a repentant heart and the other with a receptive heart bury the hatchet together.

There is a much deeper truth here than what appears on the surface. What we really have is a picture of the very way we can become plugged into our Source of power for living. There is a sense in which we are Onesimus. We are the offending party. The Creator made us to fellowship with Him. But, we chose to go our own way and leave Him out of our lives. For many years we had no relationship with Him whatsoever. He is the offended party. He provided a perfect paradise for us all. But, we thought we could do better. He, then, gave the best He had to offer and we nailed Him to a cross of execution. Yes, we offended Him. Jesus of Nazareth came into our world. Why? In order to take me, and you, by one of His nail-pierced hands and reach up to His Father, our Source, with His other hand and bring us together into a positive and productive relationship.

Is there an Onesimus reading these words? God is ready, and waiting, to receive you. He will forgive. And, what is more, He will also forget. Perhaps, in His still, small voice He may be saying to you right now, even through the words of this book, "Let's bury the hatchet. Let's start over. Let's have a brand new beginning." And, the beautiful truth is, He has already buried the hatchet…deep into a Roman cross outside the city wall of Jerusalem almost two thousand years ago. There He demonstrated His love and receptive heart toward us in reconciliation.

I stood one winter day at that very spot called Skull Hill. The largest snowfall in decades covered the landscape of Jerusalem. It was beautiful as it nestled into the crevices on the face of Calvary. The holes which form what looks like eye sockets and make Golgotha different in appearance from any other hill on earth were filled with snow. The words of the ancient Jewish prophet, Isaiah, came quickly to mind, "Come now, let us reason together," says the Lord. "Though your sins are like scarlet, they shall be as white as snow" (Is. 1:18). If you will come home to him as Onesimus came home to Philemon, He will receive you as Philemon received Onesimus and you can begin the great journey for which you were created in the first place, the eternal connection.

Corrie Ten Boom was the daughter of a Dutch watchmaker who hid Jews in their home during the days of the Nazi holocaust. As a young lady, she and her sister, Betsy, were arrested, interrogated and sent to Ravensbruck, the infamous German concentration camp. There her sister, Betsy, died. Corrie lived to tell her story in the best-selling book, *The Hiding Place* and the motion picture by the same title. She relates that years after the atrocities she was invited to speak in a church in Munich. It was there she came to face to face with him, the former Nazi who stood watch at the shower door in the processing center at Ravensbruck. She could never forget that face. Suddenly, it all flashed back...the room full of mocking, jeering men...the heaps of clothing piled in the corner...and Betsy's pained and tormented face. He approached her after the service had concluded with a radiant smile. "Fraulein," he began, "I am most grateful for your message. To think that, as you say, He has forgiven me of my sin!" He offered his hand in reconciliation. Corrie Ten Boom, who had spoken so often of the need to love and forgive, kept her own hand at her side. She says she began to think to herself as the vengeful and angry thoughts flooded her mind, "I began to see the sin of my thoughts. Jesus Christ had died for this man. Was I going to ask for more? Lord Jesus, I prayed, forgive me and help me to forgive him."

Corrie Ten Boom tried to smile at the man. She couldn't. She struggled to extend her hand. She could not. She felt nothing. No love. No warmth. She then breathed a silent prayer, "Lord Jesus, I cannot forgive him. Give me your forgiveness." She plugged into the Source! As she took his hand an incredible thing happened. Into her heart leaped a love for this stranger that was overpowering.

Corrie discovered that it is no more on our own for-giveness than it is on our own goodness that the world's healing hinges. Along with His commands to forgive others He also imparts the love to do so. Yes, we have been saying it all along. We will never be in proper relationship with others until we are in a proper relationship with ourselves and this is only possible when we tap into His love and power. Then, and only then, can we truly be about the business of...*burying the hatchet!*

Practical pointers:

Remember, burying the hatchet takes two doing their individual parts. There must be a repentant heart on the part of the offending party. There must, also, be a receptive heart on the part of the offended party. Who are you in this story?

1. Are you Onesimus, the offending party? Be honest. Is there anything in the past you have done to offend anyone? Is there anything that is left undone? Be big enough to admit it. You will never stand taller than when you go to someone and voice those two liberating words, "I'm sorry!" Perhaps, you need to write a letter, make a phone call or, better yet, pay a visit to someone and admit you were wrong. Do it for your own sake. It will set you free. After all, the way forward is still back!

2. Are you Philemon, the offended party? Be willing to forgive. Let God help you forget and go on with life. Harboring resentment will only damage you physically, depress you mentally and debilitate you spiritually. Perhaps, you need to write a letter, make a phone call or, better yet, pay a visit to someone and say, "You are forgiven!" It will set you free. It is a wonderful opportunity to pass on to someone else the forgiveness you can find in the Lord Himself.

3. Perhaps you are neither Onesimus nor Philemon. Could it be that you are Paul? What the world needs now are more men and women like Paul who play the role of reconciler. Do you know of someone who is the offending party in a relationship? Care enough about them to encourage them to see their need. Do you have a friend who is the offended party? Care enough about them to encourage them to forgive and forget, to bury the hatchet with that other person who displays genuine remorse and regret and knows how to say, "I'm sorry. Please forgive me." You could be the key. Take the initiative in playing the part of a reconciler this week with someone you know. They will thank you forever for it.

4. We only have three relationships in life. The external connection, our relationship with other people. The internal connection, our relationship with ourselves. The eternal connection, our relationship with our Maker. It may be that before you can forgive others for a particular offense you need to forgive yourself and let God love you and fill you with His power and forgiveness. The way to plug into

Him is to begin by saying, "I'm sorry. Forgive me." And, He will. He promised. And, He will go one better than that…He will forget! He will give you a brand new beginning!

Chapter 5

Crossing the Rubicon of relationships

(Philemon 17–21)

The year was 49 B.C. The order came down to Julius Caesar to disband his army and give up the struggle. He stood on the banks of the Rubicon River and pondered his dilemma. If he continued his march by crossing the river there could be no turning back. He turned to his troops, tore up his orders, and led his dedicated legion across the Rubicon to march against Rome. This act of commitment to his cause brought about a declaration of war against the Senate and, for Caesar, it paved the way for his becoming ruler of the Roman world. Since that day the phrase, "crossing the Rubicon", has been used to signify total commitment to a cause from which there can be no turning back.

There should be a Rubicon in every interpersonal relationship. That is, a line of commitment we cross from which we are "in" for the duration. Commitment is a lost word in the vocabulary of many modern relationships. Oh, some are committed alright. But, they are only committed to their own happiness. Thus, domestically, they move from relationship to relationship when their own satisfaction wanes. There is commitment at the office. But, for some, it is only a commitment to personal advancement and not to the team concept. Commitment is the missing element in many modern relationships. Not a lot of people are crossing the Rubicon of relationships today by making a commitment to one another that lasts a lifetime.

No treatise on interpersonal relationships would be complete without a word about commitment. Paul, having already addressed such vital principles as affirmation of one another, accommodation of one another and acceptance of one another, now turns his attention to the importance of allegiance to one another. He expresses his commitment to Onesimus by writing Philemon saying, "If you consider me a partner, welcome him as you would welcome me. If he has done you any wrong or owes you anything, charge it to me" (Philem.17–18). And, in the next sentence he assures Philemon of his continued commitment to him by writing, "Confident of your obedience, I write to you, knowing that you will do even more than I ask" (Philem. 21).

Lasting relationships are those which are built upon loyalty and commitment to one another. There are four steps one takes in order to cross the Rubicon of relationships. Paul articulately and accurately portrays them in his letter to his friend, Philemon. The first step is openness. It is often the most difficult. However, the longest journey begins with the first step. Commitment to one another demands openness. Committed friends have no hidden agendas and feel free to ask favors of one another. The second step is obligation. Committed friends sense an obligation to one another. They stick up for each other. There is a third step in crossing this river. It is objectivity. Committed friends are objective. They get the big picture. They see past themselves to the importance of reciprocation. They return favors. The final step is optimism. Committed friends believe the best about each other and do more than is expected in their relationships with one another. They bring out the best in each other.

Openness

Crossing this river to committed relationships begins with the step of openness. Paul is open and honest with his friend, Philemon. He writes, "So, if you consider me a partner, welcome him (Onesimus) as you would welcome me" (Philem. 17). He felt free to ask a favor. Loyal friends have a sense of openness, freedom with one another. They do not play games nor manipulate each other with hidden agendas. They are open.

One of the signal characteristics of loyal friendships which endure over the years is the element of transparency. Without openness our relationships can never get past a superficial level. Honesty and openness build lasting, positive and productive interpersonal relationships. Relationships are a risky business. Some people guard against "opening up" to anyone. There are a lot of paper faces on parade today, masks which some refuse to take off. The fear of rejection is the main culprit! Therefore, there is something within many of us which guards against becoming vulnerable to anyone else. We fear we might be rejected and consequently, we never risk a relationship and step out in openness to cross our own Rubicon.

Paul takes the step of openness with Philemon. He opens up the possibility of rejection. He takes the risk. Many will never take the risk that comes with a relationship. In fact, many spend most of their time calculating why someone else can enjoy the friendship of others and excusing why they can't. Relationships are a risky business. Ironically, the very thing we seek to keep covered up when conversing with others is the very thing, if we were open, that would attract others to us. For example, my own origins are rather humble. For a time I considered this detrimental to the development of some relationships. It sounds foolish now, but in my immaturity I sometimes sought to pretend to be someone I was not. When, at this very point, I became open with others I found that what I thought was a problem was, in reality, an asset in the development of my own interpersonal relationships. We never have to be afraid of the truth and being open with others.

As we attempt to cross the Rubicon of relationships, we do one of two things. We build bridges. Or, we build barriers. If we build more bridges over the river than we do barriers we will have more loyal and committed friends. If we build mostly barriers few will want to cross over with us.

What is being built on the construction site of your own interpersonal relationships? Barriers? Are you building barriers so that no one can look into your heart? Do you fear they might reject you if they knew what was really there? So you are busy at work building a barrier. Do you see the folly in this? I have known men and women who have been deeply hurt and rejected in the past and are in desperate need of someone to share their loyalty and love. But, they will not take the risk of being open again. So, they build barriers with others in place of bridges.

Many of us have sought to have relationships with those whom we could not penetrate. They left us feeling as though we were left out of the most intimate parts of their lives. They would not cross the Rubicon with us. The first step of openness was never taken. They built their barriers in order to hide their fears and insecurities from us. I have found in my own relational experiences that, often, those who appear to be most superior are, in reality, the least secure.

Are there any bridges being built on the construction site of your own relationships? I am not talking about letting anyone and everyone cross over into the private turf of the hidden things of the heart. I am not referring to "letting it all hang out." Openness with others is not a call for us to reveal all the sordid details of our hidden secrets. We all need our private moments. I am talking bridges here, not interstate highways. I am talking about a bridge between you and someone else. I am talking about becoming vulnerable and taking the risk of opening up with someone else. Something wonderful happens when two people connect in openness and honesty. Openness has its own way of building a bridge.

This first step of openness is what made Jesus of Nazareth so winsome in His interpersonal relationships. He was transparent. He traveled with His friends. He ate with

His friends. He prayed with His friends. He wept with His friends. He was a people person. He became involved in their struggles. He built bridges of commitment across which others could walk with Him. He allowed people to look into His heart and know Him. He told others of His own needs. And, though it was risky, for some rejected Him, many others opened up to this One who had built a bridge of openness to them.

Take the woman of Samaria, for example. She had spent a lifetime building barriers…until she met Him! Her past was smudged with many haunting moments she wished could be lived over again. She had known so much rejection that she was nearly void of any self-worth or self-respect. But, one day she met Him at a well. He built a bridge. And, she crossed over. She opened up and in so doing found a friend for life.

As Paul opens himself to Philemon he chooses an interesting Greek word in calling him a "partner". It is a word describing one mutually shared life. Paul and Philemon were connected. They were "together". Since Paul has already referred to Onesimus as "my very heart", for Philemon to now reject Onesimus would be like rejecting Paul himself. The journey back is hard enough in itself. But, it can be made more difficult by those who do not believe in the second chance.

The first step across the Rubicon of relationships is openness. We never have to be afraid of the truth! Barriers keep people out. Bridges make the way easier for others to cross the river into a life of commitment to someone else.

Obligation

The second step across this bridge to commitment is obligation. Paul senses an obligation to his trusted friend, Onesimus. He continues the letter, "If he has done you any wrong or owes you anything, charge it to me. I, Paul, am writing this with my own hand. I will pay it back" (Philem. 18–19). Loyal and committed friends stick up for one another. They are under obligation to each other. They are committed to each other and are quick to rise to each other's defense in times of need.

Paul instructs Philemon to "charge" whatever is owed him by Onesimus to his own account. Paul is in no way suggesting that Philemon forget about Onesimus' past wrongs and ignore the debt. He gives him a promissory note in his own hand with a promise to pay it. He is a committed friend. He is under an obligation that comes when we cross the Rubicon of commitment with someone else.

One of the characteristics of genuine commitment is a mutual obligation. Many bounce from relationship to relationship while always passing the blame for failure on the attitudes or actions of someone else. When a particular relationship arrives at the riverbank and it comes time to cross over in commitment, many move on to another relationship around the next corner rather than stepping out in openness and obligation. Some only want relationships where they can be on the receiving end. Commitment not only involves openness, but obligation as well. Strong relationships are built on an obligation to persevere.

There is a beautiful thing happening in this relationship between Paul and Onesimus. Paul is offering to pay a debt he doesn't owe. Why? Because Onesimus owes a debt he can not pay! Paul had nothing to do with his guilt. Yet, he assumed his debt. He says, "If he has done you any wrong, or owes you anything, charge it to me…I will repay it." Paul is a true and trusted friend. Here he shows us his openness towards Philemon and his obligation towards Onesimus.

Although this sense of paying a debt we do not owe because someone else owes a debt they can not pay is manifested in our horizontal relationships, it has its roots in our vertical relationship. There is a bit of Onesimus in each of us. We, like him, have gone our own way in rebellion against the One who loves us most. The Bible refers to what we owe our Lord as "a sin debt." We can not pay it. Just as Paul had nothing to do with Onesimus' guilt, neither does Christ with ours. And yet, as Paul assumed the debt he did not owe, so, Jesus of Nazareth made His way across His own Rubicon to a Roman cross to pay our debt. In essence, He said to His Father about you and me what Paul said to Philemon about Onesimus, "If he has done you any wrong or owes you anything, charge it to me…I will pay it back" (Philem. 18–19). It is no wonder Isaiah said, "We all, like sheep, have gone astray, each of us has turned to his own way; and the Lord has laid on him the iniquity of us all" (Is. 53:6). We are talking real commitment here. Commitment accompanied by a sense of openness and obligation. Those who have connected with their Source through Jesus Christ can go to the computer in heaven, pull up their names, look at their account, and read the words, "paid in full!"

Obligation to one another is the second step in commitment. Relationships stand strong through the years when friends stick up for one another. I remember an experience in my own life when I was falsely accused and a friend rose to my defense and took up for me. Although we have been separated from that experience by hundreds of miles and many years I have never forgotten it and a deeper bond between us resulted from it. How much more do you think Onesimus was committed to Paul after he got wind of the fact that Paul had risen so strongly to his defense? And, how much more would your friends be committed to you if you proved beyond a doubt your own commitment to them?

Objectivity

Openness and obligation are the first two steps across the Rubicon to a commitment to positive and productive interpersonal relationships. Objectivity is the third step. Paul was objective in his relationships. In his letter to Philemon, he challenges him to be likewise. He continues, "If he…owes you anything…I will pay it back — not to mention that you owe me your very self. I do wish, brother, that I may have some benefit from you in the Lord; refresh my heart in Christ" (Philem. 18–20).

Loyal friends are objective. They get the big picture. They see past themselves to realize the importance of reciprocation. They are quick to return favors. Commitment is a forgotten word in many relationships due to the fact that so many are bent on "getting" without ever "giving". True and loyal friends are objective and they bring out the best in each other.

The wave of our modern day has been a rash of faddish "self-help" books which have flooded the marketplace advocating "doing our own thing." They line the shelves of bookstores everywhere with their messages of self assertion and manipulation. They instruct about the finer points of getting leverage over the other person in the relationship. They teach how to climb to the top of the ladder of success by intimidation of others. They may increase bookstore sales but they play havoc with a lot of interpersonal relationships. One of the reasons for the current trend of short-term relationships is a lack of objectivity. Many seem to be only interested in getting, being on the receiving end of the relationship 100% of the time. Few are objective enough to see the need of reciprocation, returning favors and giving of themselves to someone else.

When our daughters were young we enjoyed taking them to the park. They loved to ride the see-saw. I can see those two toddlers on it now...up and down...up and down...up and down. Relationships have a see-saw effect. There are times in a relationship when one of the parties does most of the giving and the other most of the receiving. Then, some circumstance of life will come along and turn the tables on us and, for a while the roles will be reversed. Anyone who has been married for a long period of time knows of this law of reciprocation. For example, I know of a wife whose husband has recently lost his job. Although he doesn't verbalize it, he is having a real struggle with his own self-confidence and self-worth. He is contentious and on edge. He says some things he really doesn't mean. He is not as affectionate and giving as he normally is. The money is dwindling. Fear is setting in. Quite honestly, the wife is not "getting" much from the relationship. Some women would allow this frustration to cause them to pull away from him.

Some might even pull out. But the lady under consideration is open, obligated and objective. She realizes her husband needs her unconditional love now more than ever, even though he doesn't deserve it. So she gives. And, for a time she gives much more than she receives.

Committed friends get the big picture. They are objective. They see past themselves and their momentary needs to the importance of reciprocation. They give. They understand that friends need friends the most when they do not necessarily deserve them.

The lack of objectivity is the point of breakdown in many relationships. The need to always be receiving and never giving, the inability to see that friendship is a two-way street, are key factors in the destruction of many relationships. Get the big picture. Be a giver. Return a favor. Hop on the see-saw. There may come a time when you need to make a withdrawal on the love and concern you have deposited into someone else's account. Committed friends are objective and see the need of reciprocation in relationships.

Optimism

Paul is optimistic. He concludes his paragraph on the importance of commitment saying, "Confident of your obedience, I write to you, knowing that you will do even more than I ask" (Philem. 21). Paul is very wise and winsome. He knows how hard it is to feel good about others if we do not feel good about ourselves. He is letting Philemon know, without question, that he believes he will do the right thing. This optimistic approach has incredible results. It brings out the best in Philemon. We bring out the best in others by letting them know we are confident they will come through. Optimism is the key. Committed friends believe the best about each other and they come through in the clutch. In fact, as Paul reveals, they do more than is expected of them.

Can you imagine Philemon's emotions as he reads this letter from his trusted friend. Think about it. Paul has dropped the Onesimus bomb, laid the whole situation out, asked for a favor, and called in some chips. Having advocated the position of Philemon's adversary, he now affirms his confidence in Philemon with the assurance that he will do even more than he is asked. He lets Philemon know he believes he will do what is right…and all in advance of the fact.

Paul lets Philemon know he believes in him. He says, "I know you will do even more than I ask." There are two different Greek words he could have used to indicate this particular knowledge. One of them is indicative of a type of knowledge which comes by way of the mind through the senses. This type knowledge is grounded in personal experience. It says, "I know because I have experienced it.

I have touched it. I have smelled it. I have tasted it. Thus, I know." The other word is indicative of seeing with the mind's eye. That is, we do not have to experience it to know it is true. We just know. And, this is the word Paul chooses when he lets Philemon "know" he is optimistic he will do even more than he asks. In essence, he is saying to his friend, "I don't have to see it first. I have confidence in you. I know you will do the right thing."

Are you optimistic? Do your friends and family know you have confidence in them? Or, do you always have to experience their performance before you affirm them in some way? Susie and I have raised our daughters to young adulthood. Since the day of their birth there has not been one single day in either of their lives when they did not hear me say, "I am proud to be your dad." In a thousand ways we have sought to let them know we believe in them, we are confident they will do the right thing in life, and, in fact, we know they will do even more than we ask. Letting others know you believe in them brings out the best in them far quicker than berating them over their short-comings.

Paul does not command nor coerce Philemon to receive Onesimus. It is his call. Loyalty and commitment must be voluntary if they are to be effective. Thus, he simply presents his case, expresses his confidence in both parties and leaves the ball in Philemon's court. He knows that people have a way of becoming what we encourage them to be…not what we coerce them to be. Expecting the best in others and expressing confidence in them to do more than is expected goes a long way in helping them to do the right thing.

It is not too difficult to drown out the fires of enthusiasm. Just pour on the cold water. Throw in your two cents worth of discouragement. The whole world is full of negative pessimists. But, how many times has a simple word of confidence given someone the strength to go on? Optimism brings out the very best in everyone of us. When an athlete knows the coach believes in him he tries harder. When an employee knows the boss believes in him he works harder. When a child knows his parent believes in him he climbs higher. Optimism is what ultimately gets us across our own Rubicon of relationships.

What do you suppose Philemon did? I think he did what Paul asked and even passed on the principles to Onesimus. I think he, in turn, let Onesimus know he still believed in him. Guess what happened to this former runaway servant. History has preserved another letter written in 115 A.D. from Ignatius of Antioch to the Bishop of Ephesus. And the Bishop's name? Onesimus. Our Onesimus would have been in his seventies when the letter was received. Many scholars believe Bishop Onesimus of Ephesus was, indeed, the same Onesimus who returned to

Philemon. If so, his success and fulfillment in life was due, in large part, to the optimistic encouragement he found in his interpersonal relationships with his loyal friends, Paul and Philemon. Their commitment to one another was built on openness. They were open and honest with one another. It was built on obligation. They were unconditionally committed to one another. Their relationship was built on objectivity. They reciprocated with each other and saw past their own individual needs. Finally, their commitment to one another was built on optimism. They believed the best about each other and challenged each other to excellence.

How do you think Onesimus felt when he heard Paul rise to his defense and offer to pay his debt? He became more committed to him in their relationship to one another than ever before. How do you think Philemon felt when he discovered that Paul really believed in him? It spurred him on to a deeper commitment. There are four steps to loyal and committed friendships. Be open. Be obligated. Be objective. And, be optimistic.

Have you crossed the Rubicon with anyone? Do you have a loyal friend? One who is open to you? One who feels free to ask a favor? Do you have a friend who senses an obligation to you? One who rises to your defense and is committed to you no matter what may come? Do you have a friend who is objective about you? One who understands the importance of reciprocation and gives as much as he takes in the relationship? One who loves you when you least deserve it? Do you have a friend who is optimistic toward you? One who believes the best about you and does more than you expect in the relationship? If not, why not?

Perhaps a more pertinent question may be… "Are you a committed and loyal friend to someone else?" Are you open with others? Or, do you always keep your guard up. Do you build barriers in place of bridges? Do you sense any obligation to anyone? Or, do you base your relationships strictly on the basis of what you can get from them without ever wondering what you can give to them? Have you stood up for anyone recently? This is the cement of relationship. Are you objective? Or, do you soon forget the investment someone else makes in your life? Are you slow at reciprocation and returning favors? Are you optimistic? Do you believe the best about others? Or, are you suspicious of their motives?

Where can we begin to build more positive relationships? It all goes back to being well connected at the source. That is, being plugged into spiritual power. We all have a friend who "sticks closer than a brother." Jesus Christ is committed to you. He is open. His life is an open book. He builds bridges and not barriers.

He also builds relationships on obligation. He stands

up for you. He crossed his own Rubicon for you and never looked back. He is committed. He is objective. He is no respecter of persons. And, He is optimistic. He always does more than is expected. He brings out the best in us. He believes in us and helps us to believe in ourselves.

Commitment is a lost word in the vocabulary of many people. There is a Rubicon in every interpersonal relationship, a river we cross from which there is no turning back or quitting. Many move up to the banks of this relational river with someone but never cross over. It takes four steps to get across. We must become open with one another. True commitment is based on openness, the ability to be honest and to take a risk. We must sense our obligations to each other. True commitment causes us to rise to each other's defense. We must be objective. Reciprocation is the name of the relationship game. We must be optimistic. When we believe in someone else we bring out the best in them. Genuine commitment results in our...*crossing the Rubicon!*

Practical pointers:

Most of us know a lot about commitment. We are committed to our jobs. We show up on time and do an honest day's work because we have made a commitment. Some of us enjoy the fellowship found in all sorts of endeavors from bowling teams to garden clubs. We show up because we made a commitment. Many of us are in civic or social clubs. When we miss a meeting we "make it up." We are committed. It is time some of us made the same commitment to an interpersonal relationship.

Do something for someone this week. In Paul's words, "Refresh someone's heart." Do a favor that is unsolicited. Loyalty breeds loyalty in relationships. Pay someone a sincere compliment. A few suggestions follow.

1. Refresh the heart of someone who regularly serves you at a particular restaurant this week. Pay an honest and optimistic compliment. Rise to their defense.

2. Refresh the heart of your husband or wife. Be objective. Perhaps it has been too long since you reciprocated in the relationship. Give. Don't just always receive. Do something "out of character" for him or her this week. Buy her some flowers. Write him a letter and stick it in his briefcase before he leaves on a business trip.

3. Refresh your child's heart this week. Many of us dads are committed to a lot of things…except fatherhood. Think about that. Have you crossed the Rubicon to make a commitment to fatherhood or motherhood? Let your child know you are proud of them and that you believe in them. This optimistic spirit will help bring out the best in them and, in turn, cause them to be more committed to you than ever before.

4. Refresh a friend's heart this week. Take a risk. Be open. Let someone look into your own heart. Build a bridge. Honesty and openness will get you started on the way across your own Rubicon of relationships. Believe in someone…and let them know it!

5. Be open. Be obligated. Be objective. Be optimistic. Go ahead, cross the Rubicon of relationships.

Chapter 6

Accountability: Don't leave home without it!

(Philemon 22–25)

I am an All-American boy. Part of the proof is in the fact that I drive American-made automobiles. One of the reasons I do is because of the super service department at my local dealership. Periodically, I take my car in for a check-up. The service manager makes certain my automobile is properly maintained so that it will continue to run smoothly with minimal mechanical maladies.

Like many of my readers, my wife and I are fortunate enough to own our home. Or, I should say the mortgage holder owns it. Periodically, we give it a check-up. Recently, we made some repairs on the roof. It wasn't leaking…yet! Some wood was rotting around one of the eaves and it was only a matter of time before big problems would ensue. So, we did some preventive maintenance.

I have a body. Not much of one, some might argue! But, a body never-the-less. Every year I go to my physician, Dr. Ken Cooper, for a check-up. I get a complete physical in order to make certain everything is in proper working order and to, hopefully, detect any possible problems. Along with a physical exam I watch my diet and try to take good physical care of myself. It is called preventive medicine.

Much of what goes wrong with my car or my home or my body does so because of one word...*neglect*. No check-up. No maintenance. No accountability. Accountability. Now, that is an important word. If it is good enough for cars and homes and physical needs, why shouldn't it be good enough for interpersonal relationships? It is good from time to time for husbands and wives to sit down with each other and "check-up" on their relationships to one another. It is good from time to time for parents and their children to sit down and hold each other accountable in the relationship. It is good from time to time for friends to stop long enough to do some preventive maintenance with their interpersonal relationships.

Paul closes his letter to Philemon by letting him know he will hold him accountable in the relationship and will come by later for a check-up. He writes, "And one thing more: Prepare a guest room for me, because I hope to be restored to you in answer to your prayers"(Philem. 22). Philemon knew what this meant. Paul was going to come by later to checkup on the relationship! Philemon knew he would be held accountable. Paul was a wise man. He knew much of what goes wrong in relationships does so because of neglect. No accountability. No check-ups. No maintenance in the relationships.

Accountability is a part of life. We all need it. We need accountability in the marriage relationship. Marriages that last are those which have some preventive maintenance. When accountability goes, relationships go with it. I am accountable to my wife. I do not just go my own way telling her that where I go and what I do is none of her business. It is her business. We are one. We have a unique relationship because we are accountable to one another for what we do, where we go and how we behave.

We all know about accountability. We have it at the office. We do not just show up at work on Monday morning whenever we so desire. We must be there at a certain time and work a certain number of hours if we expect to get paid. Some of us are accountable for quotas and the like. Profitable businesses are successful in large part due to the insistence upon accountability at the office.

Look at our national, state and local governments. We

have accountability here. As citizens we need laws to govern and protect us. We need to be held accountable if we run through stop signs and break speed limits. Without accountability in government there would be total anarchy. Accountability is a part of our everyday life. We are faced with it in some way at every turn of the corner.

We have accountability in our schools. Teachers hold students accountable with their studies. They must turn in home work assignments, write certain papers and take scheduled tests. No one graduates or earns a degree without being held accountable for the required assignments. Accountability is a way of life for all of us.

What about the athletic arena? We have accountability there also. If an athlete refuses to attend practice sessions, he or she doesn't play in the game. And, for example, in basketball, when a player commits five "fouls" in a single game he is taken out of the game by the official. Athletes are accountable to officials, umpires and referees on the playing field.

Accountability is all around us. We see it in the business world. Many of us have mortgages with scheduled monthly payments. We are held accountable to pay them promptly and on time. If we fail to do so we are in danger of foreclosure.

Accountability is a significant part of everything we do.

It is strange that, although we have accountability in every aspect of life, when we come to our own interpersonal relationships with our friends we do not see the need of it. Is it any wonder there is an epidemic of short-term relationships today? If accountability is necessary in government, athletics, education, business and the like, it is also essential in developing lasting positive and productive friendships.

When I was a teenager a friend by the name of Jack Graham and I began to take note of what was happening around us. We watched some of our peers disintegrate and destroy their young lives through such things as alcohol, drugs and illicit sex. Jack and I became accountable to one another. We didn't know what to call it, but we made a promise to God and to each other that we would help one another to stay clean. We checked up weekly on one another and held each other accountable. To this day, although we began almost forty years ago, he is still my best friend and we still have a relationship that involves personal accountability to one another.

What destroys relationships? Think about it. The answer is found in such attitudes as self-reliance, self-righteousness, self-sufficiency and self-centeredness. Accountability is an absolute necessity in the building of long-term friendships. Over the long haul it is one of the most important factors in a relationship. The lack of it has been the downfall of a lot of potential and promise. Accountability is the "ability" to be open and allow a small number of trusted, loyal and committed friends to speak the truth in love to us. We should only be accountable to those who have our best interest at heart. We all are in need of someone from whom we can receive concerned counsel and correction.

Accountability is a word many of us fear. It is not in our nature to want to be held accountable for our attitudes or actions. Some of us fear it because we misunderstand it. We think it means only "put-downs", criticisms or rebukes from those who take delight in sitting in the judge's seat. Remember, we are talking about the accountability that comes from a very select few trusted, loyal and committed friends who want only the best for us. Relationships are doomed to defeat without the element of accountability. We all need it.

Accountability in interpersonal relationships calls for three things. First, insight. Paul closes his letter to Philemon by reminding him he is coming by to checkup on how things are going between him and Onesimus. Hindsight also plays a major role in accountability. It involves an investment of time and interest. We need the hindsight to see that every area of positive relationships (affirmation, accommodation, acceptance and allegiance to one another) are important. I am not going to make myself accountable to someone who is not a trusted friend and who does not have my best interests at heart. Accountability also calls for foresight. Paul concludes his letter with the hope that "grace" might rest upon his trusted friend. We need the foresight to see that we all need a little grace to make any relationship positive and productive. Accountability. We all need it. Don't leave home without it!

Insight

We now arrive at the final paragraph of this enlightening letter on interpersonal relationships. I can almost see Philemon now, with chin cupped in hand, as he reads, "And one thing more: Prepare a guest room for me, because I hope to be restored to you in answer to your prayers" (Philem. 22). Paul is a bit subtle here. But the message is loud and clear. "I am going to come by to checkup on you. Get the guest room ready! I am coming by to see how you and Onesimus are doing in your relationship." Here is *accountability* in capital letters.

How do you think this motivated Philemon? The prospect of Paul's upcoming visit no doubt speeded up the process of his doing the right thing in his relationship with the remorseful Onesimus. We all need accountability to help us do what we ought to do. When we speak of holding each other accountable we are not speaking of making threats. Some confuse the two. Paul does not say, "Unless you do what I have asked you to do, I am not coming by to see you any more." Men and women who endure relationships built upon threats base their friendships upon performance. Not Paul. He builds relationships on such things as affirmation, forgiveness, commitment and accountability.

There is a subtle insight into this letter that is only apparent when it is read in its original Greek form. He requests that Philemon, "Prepare a guest room for me, because I hope to be restored to you in answer to your prayers." The "you" and "your" are both plural. This is both subtle and significant. Paul is reminding Philemon that others will be watching. Consequently, we discover the insight that accountability calls for us to become transparent, touchable, teachable and truthful.

Accountability with one another calls for the insight to see we must be *transparent* with our true friends. Everyone needs someone with whom they can be genuinely open, honest and transparent. This vulnerability carries with it the risk of being wounded. But, transparency is imperative to accountability.

Those who are accountable must also be *touchable*. Everyone needs someone whom they can touch. That is, someone who is accessible and approachable. To his Roman friends Paul later wrote, "You are full of goodness, complete in knowledge and competent to instruct one another." To his friends in Galatia he wrote, "Let us not become conceited, provoking and envying one another...carry each other's burdens." To be accountable to someone demands that we become not only transparent, but, also, touchable.

Relationships which profit from accountability do so because the parties involved are also *teachable*. None of us should ever stop learning. We have so much to learn from one another. It is a dangerous time in any interpersonal relationship when someone feels they know it all and no longer possesses a teachable spirit. This insight implies a spirit of humility. We can teach each other. We can learn from one another. We need each other. King Solomon, the wisest man who ever lived, said, "As iron sharpens iron, so one man sharpens another" (Prov. 27:17).

Those who are accountable to one another must not only be transparent, touchable and teachable, they must also be *truthful*. Many never allow themselves to enter an accountable relationship because of deception. They are so deceived in the thinking process that they are convinced it is always someone else's fault when a relationship becomes bruised or broken. Many people have left dozens of broken relationships in their wake and, in their minds, they have not been responsible for the break-up of a single one.

They are deceived. Without truthfulness there can be no accountability in our relationships.

Some men and women are never accountable in their relationships because of denial. Some simply live in a state of denial. Still others are never accountable because they live in defeat. Everyone needs someone with whom they can be truthful. It is extremely therapeutic to be able to be genuinely truthful with a faithful friend without the fear that he or she will reveal your innermost secrets of the heart. It is impossible to become accountable to one another unless we are both committed to the truth, whoever or whatever it may hurt. We never have to be afraid of the truth. It liberates. It sets us free.

For example, take the well known case of King David and his mistress, Bathsheba. Like so many today, he tried his best to cover up his affair with her. He did not want his family or friends to know about it. David was fortunate in that he had a trusted friend who held him accountable. Nathan cared enough to confront his friend who was on a collision course. And, he did so in confidence and in love. David came clean. When he was confronted with the truth, it hurt. But, it also healed. Nathan held his friend accountable and it kept the king from greater hurt and heartache. It worked because in their relationships with one another they were transparent, touchable, teachable and truthful.

Many of us have personal friends we see heading down a road that has a dead end. But we let them go. We do not really care enough to confront with compassion. We have little accountability in relationships today. Real friends hold real friends accountable. How? By being transparent, touchable, teachable and truthful with one another.

WARNING! We are not talking about open season here. We are not advocating opening up our lives to anyone and everyone. And, in particular, we are not talking about becoming accountable to those who boast of the gifts of criticism, gossip or judgment. Stay away from those folks. They do not have your best interest at heart. They will end up hurting you a lot more than they will help you. We are talking about accountability between a small number of loyal, affirmative, forgiving and committed friends who, like Paul, have earned the right to ask some hard questions. Solomon also said, "Wounds from a friend can be trusted, but an enemy multiplies kisses" (Prov. 27:6).

Accountability calls for insight. Paul lets Philemon know he is coming by to check up on him. We all need a measure of accountability. There is something about knowing that we will one day have to give account of ourselves that motivates us to be more conscientious about our task. We all need someone with whom we can be transparent, touchable, teachable and truthful.

Hindsight

Accountability becomes possible when we have the hindsight to see we have made an investment of time and interest in another's life which earns us the right to hold them accountable. And, to be accountable ourselves. Paul continues his closing paragraph by sending Philemon greetings from five of their mutual friends, a somewhat subtle reminder of those with whom he and Philemon have had solid and mutually beneficial relationships in the past. He writes, "Epaphras sends you greetings and so do Mark, Aristarchus, Demas and Luke, my fellow workers."

Paul, in hindsight, mentions five individuals here. They are not recalled at random. They are each mentioned for a definite purpose. He is a genius at the art of connecting. He has dealt with five major contributions to positive inter-personal relationships…affirmation, accommodation, acceptance, allegiance and accountability. Each of these men is mentioned, in hindsight, to illustrate what he has been driving home throughout his personal correspondence to Philemon. Each man is representative of a paragraph in the letter and of a chapter in this book.

For example, he began the letter with the importance of affirmation, a pat on the back. It is no coincidence that he now brings up the name of Aristarchus. He was Paul's traveling companion on his third missionary journey throughout the Mediterranean world and was arrested when they were in Ephesus. He had been through thick and thin with Paul. He went all the way to Rome with him affirming him all along the way. Paul reveals they had a synergy together that was strengthened by their affirmation of one another.

Paul also mentions a man named Luke. Dr. Luke, we might call him. In his letter to the Colossians, Paul refers to Luke as his "dear friend and doctor." Paul brings him up in hindsight to Philemon to remind him of the win-win philosophy of relationships mentioned earlier in the letter. Paul and Luke played win-win with each other. Luke was a Gentile. In that day most Jews, like Paul, would have had no dealings with him. But Paul and Luke had something to offer each other and found their friendship to be mutually beneficial. Luke accompanied Paul on his second missionary journey and tended to his physical needs which were many. There is no doubt that Luke's health skills added years to Paul's life. They traveled a lot of miles together. On more than one occasion Paul was stoned and left for dead. He had a physical malady many believe was either epilepsy or failing eyesight. Luke was always there by his side. They needed each other. If there ever was a win-win relationship in life it was the one between Paul and Luke. Philemon knew about this and the moment he read Luke's name he thought about Paul's words a few paragraphs earlier, "He is now profitable both to you and to me. We all can win."

Paul has also made much of the necessity of forgiveness in our relationships. Thus, he mentions a man named Mark. It was young Mark who was with him on the first journey departing from Antioch. But, he failed. He quit. He went A.W.O.L. when the going got tough. Twelve years have now passed and this is the first mention of Mark in any of Paul's writings. Obviously, they have buried the hatchet and he is back. And, in case there is any doubt in anyone's mind whether their new relationship flourished, Paul mentions him in a later letter to Timothy saying, "Only Luke is with me. Get Mark and bring him with you, because he is helpful to me." Mark knew what it meant to be accountable and he knew what it meant to be forgiven. Paul's forgiveness and insistence upon accountability paid off in the end. Mark is the author of the Gospel which bears his name. Oh, the mention of his name spoke volumes to Philemon's heart as he continued to read this letter. In hindsight, he had no option but to restore his broken friendship with his former friend who was on his way home.

Paul has also talked about the need of commitment in our interpersonal relationships, the need to cross the Rubicon. Therefore, it comes as no surprise he mentions Epaphras. This man's life was characterized by a total commitment to his friends. In the Colossian letter Paul says, "Epaphras...sends his greetings. He is always wrestling in prayer for you, that you may stand firm in all the will of God, mature and fully assured. I vouch for him that he is working hard for you and for those at Laodicia and Hierapolis." He so crossed the Rubicon of relationship with Paul that he went to Rome and voluntarily shared Paul's imprisonment with him there. He was also a well-known friend of Philemon coming from the same city. His very name is synonymous with commitment. Philemon knew where Paul was coming from the moment he read his name.

Finally, Paul reminds Philemon, and us, that accountability plays a vital role in any long-term positive and productive relationship. Therefore, he mentions a man named Demas. Demas' own story ends on a lamentable note. Paul writes in his second letter to Timothy, "Demas, because he loved this world, has deserted me and has gone to Thessalonica." Demas is a sad commentary on the fact that without accountability long-term relationships have little hope of survival. By mentioning these five mutual friends, each representative of an area of positive relationships, Paul is reminding us all that we need each other. We not only need to be connected with our Source and with ourselves, but, we need to be connected with each other. We need support and strength.

In hindsight, we see this principle of accountability was what Paul effectively and continually used to develop his productive and mutually beneficial relationships. It takes hindsight to see that accountability is based on loyalty to one another. I do not intend to make myself accountable to someone who does not have my best interest at heart. Paul had a small group around him who were committed to one another and bent on affirming one another daily. This is not only what the world needs now, it is what you and I need now. To understand accountability we need insight and hindsight. We also need foresight.

Foresight

Paul concludes his letter to Philemon with a benediction, "The grace of the Lord Jesus Christ be with your spirit." What is his point? We must have the foresight to see we need grace and without it there is no hope of accountability in interpersonal relationships. Too many never become accountable to anyone else because of a warped idea of what it really is. Some equate accountability with judgment when it is intended to be equated with grace. Paul is not talking about judging one another's faults here. He is talking about mercy and grace issuing out of mutual love and respect among friends.

Grace…that is what is needed in so many relationships

today. Grace can be defined as unmerited favor. While mercy is not getting what we do deserve, grace is getting what we do not deserve! And, if it is good enough to receive from our Source of love and power, the Lord Himself, it is good enough to pass on to those around us. This is the key that unlocks the door to accountability. We all need the foresight to see that we need grace in our relationships for without it there is no hope of building positive interpersonal relationships with anyone. If I make a mistake in my own relationships I always seek to err on the side of grace and mercy rather than on the side of judgment.

Paul is making it plain to Philemon that if he is going to do what he is being called upon to do with Onesimus he is going to need an extra portion of grace to accomplish it. It is really not in us to forgive and forget. Onesimus is on his way home. Philemon knows he must receive him and forgive him and now he is reminded that it will take the grace of God to do that. God's grace…that is what we all need in our interpersonal relationships. We need the grace to go forward and the foresight to see we can not do it in our own strength. Yes, until we are properly connected at the source we will spend a lifetime trying to build relationships without grace. And it can not be done.

Paul asked that the grace of God be with Philemon's "spirit". This is by design and not by accident. We are made of body, soul and spirit. My spirit is the real me. It is that part of me that makes me different from all the other created order. It is that part of me that can connect with God. It is my inner self. We need the foresight to see that if we are not connected with our source in the spiritual realm we will never be properly connected with others in the emotional or physical realm. We need this grace to live in long-term interpersonal relationships. Husbands and wives need grace in their accountability towards one another. Friends in the marketplace need grace to get through the week. From time to time we all need grace, we all need to get what we do not necessarily deserve. Accountability can not exist without a measure of grace.

With this reminder about grace Paul closes this most intimate and personal letter on interpersonal relationships. It is a word for us although it is removed by two millennia and 8,000 miles. It is as up-to-date as any best selling book on relationships in the marketplace today. It calls to mind the life-changing method of a simple pat on the back. It brings us into win-win relationships with our friends. It speaks of the necessity of burying some hatchets along the way. It calls upon us to cross the Rubicon of relationships by making a life commitment to each other. And, it concludes with the importance of accountability to one another. We need each other.

If a periodic check-up is important to the maintenance of my automobile, my home and my physical body, why isn't it good enough for my interpersonal relationships? Much of what goes wrong with my car, my home or my body does so because of one word... "neglect!" No accountability. No check-up. No maintenance. Accountability is a part of life. We all need it desperately. The knowledge that someone is going to hold us accountable motivates us to do the right thing. Paul is coming by to check up on Philemon. The anticipation of this would spur Philemon on to obey the wishes he found in his personal letter from his trusted friend.

We come to the end of the letter. And, the end of the volume in hand. What happened? Did Philemon do what Paul asked? Did he receive Onesimus with open arms as a "dear brother"? Did he forgive? Did he forget? The answer to these questions is shrouded in silence. Quite honestly, we do not know. But, these are not really the pertinent questions for us. The question is not, "What did Philemon do?" The question is, "What will you do with the Onesimus in your own life?" The issue has been left unanswered so that you may finish the story. It will take grace to do that. We conclude as we began. We will never be properly related to each other until we possess a positive self-image and self-respect. And we will never be properly related to ourselves until we discover how indescribably valuable we are to God by becoming properly connected to Him. This has always been, and, will always be, the bottom line in…*the art of connecting!*

Practical pointers:

Be honest…with yourself. How many long-term relationships do you have? Think about it. How many friends have you kept across the years? Do your relationships suffer from neglect? Neglect your car long enough and there will come the morning when it will not start. Neglect your house long enough and there will come the day when the roof will leak. Neglect your body long enough and there will come the day it too will break down. Neglect your interpersonal relationships and, like everything else in life, they, too, will disintegrate. We all need accountability in our relationships. Remember, there are only three relationships in life. The outward expression, our relationship with others. The inward expression, our relationship with the self. And, the upward expression, our relationship with God. Accountability is called for in all three expressions.

1. We need accountability with others in the outward expression of relationships. Stop building barriers. Build a bridge to someone this week. How? Give them a pat on the back. Bury a hatchet with someone. Learn to say, "I am sorry." Or, "I forgive you." Then, forget it. Make a conscious decision to cross your own Rubicon with someone. Be vulnerable. You need accountability with someone you can trust. When you find him or her, then become transparent, touchable, teachable and truthful. We really do need each other.

2. We need accountability with ourselves in the inward expression of relationships. Make an honest self inventory of your past relationships. Could it be, even the most remote possibility, that you are to blame for some of your own failed relationships in the past? Take some personal responsibility. Be accountable to yourself. List some things you could do differently to improve your relationships. Put them into practice with someone this week. Stop fooling yourself. It may not always be the other person's fault. And, by the way, forgiveness should not always be extended to just the other party. Sometimes it should be extended to ourselves. Forgive yourself and move on!

3. Ultimately, we will all be accountable to God in the upward expression of relationships. Yes, there will come a day when everyone "must give an account of himself to God." In anticipation of this day there are three important questions you should ask yourself when you arrive at some of the confusing intersections of life. First, ask yourself, "Can I do it in Jesus name?" The Bible, the greatest book on interpersonal relationships ever written, says, "Whatever you do, do it in the name of Jesus." There are a lot of past decisions we wished had been averted that would have been if we had asked that question before the light turned green and we made a wrong turn. A second question is — "Can I thank God for it?" That is, when it is all over, can I look back and thank God for the decision I made? The Bible says, "In everything give thanks." Finally, ask yourself, "Can I do it for God's glory?" Paul admonished those at Corinth in his letter to them that "whether you eat or drink or whatever you do, do it all for the glory of God" (1 Cor. 10:31). Have the foresight to see that even though you may neglect the need for accountability with others in relationships or even with yourself, you will, ultimately, be accountable to the One who loves you most and gave Himself for you. Get connected to Him through faith in the Lord Jesus Christ and you will awaken to a brand new you. Positive and productive interpersonal relationships will then be but a by-product in...*the art of connecting!*

Appendix A

"The letter"

A.D. 60

Dear Philemon:

Paul, a prisoner of Christ Jesus, and Timothy our brother, to Philemon our dear friend and fellow worker, to Apphia our sister, to Archippus our fellow soldier and to the church that meets in your home: Grace to you and peace from God our Father and the Lord Jesus Christ.

I always thank my God as I remember you in my prayers, because I hear about your faith in the Lord Jesus and your love for all the saints. I pray that you may be active in sharing your faith, so that you will have a full understanding of every good thing we have in Christ. Your love has given me great joy and encouragement, because you, brother, have refreshed the hearts of the saints.

Therefore, although in Christ I could be bold and order you to do what you ought to do, yet I appeal to you on the basis of love. I then, as Paul — an old man and now also a prisoner of Christ Jesus — I appeal to you for my son Onesimus, who became my son while I was in chains. Formerly he was useless to you, but now he has become useful both to you and to me.

I am sending him — who is my very heart — back to you. I would have liked to keep him with me so that he could take your place in helping me while I am in chains for the gospel. But I did not want to do anything without your consent, so that any favor you do will be spontaneous and not forced. Perhaps the reason he was separated from you for a little while was that you might have him back for good — no longer as a slave, but better than a slave, as a dear brother. He is very dear to me but even dearer to you, both as a man and as a brother in the Lord.

So if you consider me a partner, welcome him as you would welcome me. If he has done you any wrong or owes you anything, charge it to me. I, Paul, am writing this with my own hand. I will pay it back — not to mention that you owe me your very self. I do wish, brother, that I may have some benefit from you in the Lord; refresh my heart in Christ. Confident of your obedience, I write to you, knowing that you will do even more than I ask.

And one thing more: Prepare a guest room for me, because I hope to be restored to you in answer to your prayers.

Epaphras, my fellow prisoner in Christ Jesus, sends you greetings. And so do Mark, Aristarchus, Demas and Luke, my fellow workers. The grace of the Lord Jesus Christ be with your spirit.

Sincerely,

Paul

Appendix B

Become a lifelong partner with GuideStone Financial Resources

If you serve in a Southern Baptist church these paragraphs are unapologetically for you and they could be some of the most important paragraphs you will read. Although you will never "retire" from ministry there will come a day when you will retire from vocational church service.

It is important to get started early in retirement planning. There is a thing called compound interest, which is extremely powerful. For example, assuming an 8% annual return, if a twenty-five year old minister put $50 per month in his retirement account it would be worth $174,550 at age sixty-five. If the same person waited until just the age of thirty-five to begin saving for retirement with the same $50 per month it would be worth $74,520 at age sixty-five, a difference of $100,000. It is very important to start early, but it is also important to start wherever you are along the way to retirement.

The beautiful and beneficial part of being in the Guide-Stone retirement program is the protection section. Did you know that if you or your church contributes only a few dollars per month to your retirement you automatically receive at no cost a survivor's benefit worth up to $100,000 to whomever you designate as your beneficiary? You also receive at no cost a $500 per month disability benefit simply by being a part of the GuideStone retirement program. This benefit is a cooperative effort provided by your state Baptist convention and GuideStone and is a safety net every church should utilize for their ministers.

We at GuideStone want to be a lifelong partner with you throughout your entire ministry. This is the driving reason behind products which give you additional opportunities to save for retirement, or whatever your saving needs. You have available to you savings vehicles in addition to your regular 403(b) plan that includes Personal Investing Accounts and IRAs (Traditional and Roth IRAs). These opportunities are also available to spouses of persons eligible to participate in GuideStone plans. Perhaps you have a retirement accumulation in a 401(k) plan from a previous employer. You may want to consider "rolling over" that accumulation into your retirement account or into a rollover IRA.

For more information about these new personal investing products, matching contributions from your state conventions, the protection section at no cost, housing allowance advantages in retirement, our mission church assistance fund, our relief ministries or any of our other services, visit us on the World Wide Web at *www.GuideStone.org* or better yet call us at **1-800-262-0511** and speak personally to one of our Customer Relations Specialists.